MICHAEL NAYA

WAR+MEDIC HERO

A portrait of Sergeant Pierre Naya

MILITARY MEDAL RAMC

MICHAEL NAYA

WAR+MEDIC
HERO

A portrait of Sergeant Pierre Naya

MILITARY MEDAL RAMC

MEMOIRS

Cirencester

Mereo Books

1A The Wool Market Dyer Street Cirencester Gloucestershire GL7 2PR
An imprint of Memoirs Publishing www.mereobooks.com

War medic hero: 978-1-86151-241-3

First published in Great Britain in 2014
by Mereo Books, an imprint of Memoirs Publishing

Copyright ©2014

Michael Naya has asserted his right under the Copyright Designs and Patents
Act 1988 to be identified as the author of this work.

A CIP catalogue record for this book is available from the British Library.

The address for Memoirs Publishing Group Limited can be found at www.memoirspublishing.com

The Memoirs Publishing Group Ltd Reg. No. 7834348

The Memoirs Publishing Group supports both The Forest Stewardship Council® (FSC®) and the PEFC®
leading international forest-certification organisations. Our books carrying both the FSC label and the
PEFC® and are printed on FSC®-certified paper. FSC® is the only
forest-certification scheme supported by the leading environmental organisations including Greenpeace.
Our paper procurement policy can be found at www.memoirspublishing.com/environment

Typeset in 12/18pt Plantin
by Wiltshire Associates Publisher Services Ltd. Printed and bound in Great Britain by Printondemand-
Worldwide, Peterborough PE2 6XD

To my beloved brother Pierre
1945-2012
Rest in peace

To Nina, his beloved wife, and his daughters
Juliette, Ginette, Alison and Nicola

ACKNOWLEDGEMENTS

My sincere thanks to Peter and Kay for your help in writing this book. Peter, you have been my rock, always listening and pointing the way forward when I needed it.

With warm thanks to my wife Barbara for putting up with my endless hours at the computer and for her cups of tea and words of wisdom.

My warm thanks also to Max Arthur OBE, author of Above All, Courage, and his publishers, Orion Publishing Company. Excerpts from Pierre's narrative were taken from this book, first published in 1985.

Also my grateful thanks to Col. Jim Ryan for his foreword to this book about a very brave and honest human being, my brother and hero Pierre Naya, Royal Army Medical Corp.

CONTENTS

Foreword

Introduction

FOREWORD

By Col. Jim Ryan

It is a unique privilege to be invited to write the foreword to this remarkable and very personal narrative. It is a book first and foremost for those who work as military medics. But it deserves a much wider audience, particularly those, whether military or humanitarian, who have had experience of war and catastrophes. Politicians might fruitfully peruse the pages of the book to help them understand the real world consequences of the actions they so easily take.

At its centre is the story of an undisputed war hero, Pierre Naya, a larger-than-life character of the sort few get a chance to rub shoulders with. However, it paints a much broader canvas. Wrapped around the story of Pierre is a wider story of two remarkable men and their family – the Nayas. It puts Pierre into the context of his wider life, his beginnings and his odyssey through his early life in Tanzania, his abrupt departure for the United Kingdom and his new life as a medic in the Royal Army Medical Corps (RAMC). This would position him in the right place and at the right time to be deployed as a senior Operating Theatre Technician (OTT) with 55 Field Surgical Team to the Falkland Islands in the spring of 1982.

But let us step back to an earlier time – the 1960s. The Naya boys' father, Jules Naya, was born in 1915 in the former British colony of the Seychelles – a group of beautiful islands in the middle of the Indian

Ocean, 1500 miles south-east of the East African coast. Like so many of his contemporaries he was forced to emigrate to find work and care for his family, so he moved to the then Crown Colony of Tanganyika – formerly the German colony of German East Africa. In the early part of the book Michael Naya, the author, paints a picture of an idyllic life in Colonial Tanganyika. Mike describes in a colourful way their time in Dar es Salaam – school days, fishing and hunting trips and, above, their love of music.

Sadly, after independence the political scene changed and the non-African immigrant family were forced to leave, abandoning their house and leaving with very few possessions. A sadly all too familiar story. The family moved to the UK with their few possessions. Both Pierre and Mike joined the British Army and elected to join the RAMC. From then on their paths merged and separated but both would qualify as OTTs and achieve high rank. By 1982 Pierre was a Staff Sergeant and senior OTT and ripe for duty in a war zone, where our paths would meet. Mike Naya describes in fascinating detail our trip to war in a large cruise liner converted to a troop carrier role. It seemed like a holiday adventure, but that would soon change.

Pierre and the author of this foreword were part of a unique unit with its origins in the Western Desert of World War 2. It was called 55 Field Surgical Team or 55 FST, and consisted of two field surgical teams. Pierre was the senior OTT with one of these teams, the author a surgeon with the other team.

Fatefully 55 FST would embark on the Landing ship Sir Galahad. The book describes in harrowing detail the subsequent bombing and the heroic behaviour of the man at the centre of this tale - Pierre. For his heroism Pierre was awarded the coveted Military Medal. For the remainder of the war he carried out his duties with the FST in exemplary fashion and at the war's end he and the author and their teams were positioned in the Falkland Islands' only hospital – the King Edward the VII Memorial Hospital. It was here that this writer came to see at first hand all Pierre's extraordinary qualities, so eloquently described by the author in the opening section of this book. His generosity of spirit, his cheerfulness and his musical ability shone brightly and cheered all of us on. What we did not know at the time was that Pierre was suffering greatly in silence as a consequence of what he had seen in the bowels of the burning ship. The sights and sounds of men screaming in agony and terror and the dead and dying were eating into him. He never showed these feelings, and sadly we did not notice.

The author then goes on to describe the cost of his brother's heroism – sadness and depression manifested as post-traumatic stress disorder. To add insult to injury we hear of the Home Office attempt to remove his citizenship when Pierre applied to have his passport, lost on Sir Galahad, replaced. Only after years of anxiety would this be resolved. A heart-breaking story, but all too credible.

One puts this book down at once gasping in awe of Pierre. With the love of his wife Nina and his lovely daughters, Pierre gained a degree of solace and was able to enjoy his later years in retirement in the Algarve and return to his fishing and music. He died too young of heart disease, but we who were privileged to know him are left with memories of a unique gentle giant and a true war hero.

Colonel (Rtd.) J M Ryan OBE OStJ
Emeritus Professor of Conflict & Catastrophe Medicine
St George's University of London

INTRODUCTION

Pierre Naya, my brother, was awarded the Military Medal for his brave actions and heroic deeds whilst serving as a medic in the Falklands Islands War as part of the task force in 1982. The Military Medal (MM) was, until 1993 when it was discontinued, awarded to ranks below commissioned officers for bravery in battle. It was established in 1916. It was the "other rank" equivalent to the Military Cross (MC). Since 1993 its replacement has been the Military Cross for bravery.

The Military Medal is a circular silver medal of 36mm diameter. The reverse has the inscription "FOR BRAVERY IN THE FIELD" in four lines surrounded by a laurel wreath surmounted by the Royal Cypher and Imperial Crown. The obverse bears the effigy of the reigning monarch. The ribbon is dark blue, 1.25 inches wide, with five equal centre stripes of white, red, white, red and white 0.125 inches each. His citation reads:

AWARD OF THE MILITARY MEDAL 23952578
SERGEANT NAYA PHR "PIERRE"
ROYAL ARMY MEDICAL CORP JUNE 1982

While at anchor in Fitzroy Sound on June 8 1982, RFA Sir Galahad was bombed and set on fire by enemy aircraft. Embarked troops included two companies of infantry and the main body of 16 Field Ambulance, men and equipment.

At the time of the attack most of the troops were positioned in the tank deck, where substantial quantities of ammunition soon began to explode as the fire worked through the ship. Over the course of some two hours 135 casualties, the majority with burns and amputations, were evacuated to the Advanced Dressing Station already ashore at Fitzroy settlement.

Sergeant Naya, Royal Army Medical Corp, was standing in the tank deck when he was thrown against a bulkhead by the first explosion and partially stunned. The lights went out and the tank deck began to fill with dense black smoke. A second explosion killed two men behind him, set his large pack alight and scorched the back of his head. Shrugging off the burning material, he managed to lead a third soldier by hand up two flights of stairs to daylight. There he paused to cut burning clothing from other soldiers with his scissors before mounting a third flight to the upper deck. He then helped to carry a man who had lost his a leg up to the forecastle, having first administered first aid and set up intravenous infusion. He treated many more casualties, included another amputee, and set up several more infusions, until all casualties had been evacuated, he left the ship on the last helicopter, later to be evacuated as a casualty himself. After only three days he returned to duty in the Advance Surgical Centre of the field ambulance, where he worked steadfastly through the most intense period of military activity and the passage of many battle casualties.

Pierre, as a casualty himself, was well aware of the dangers he faced by remaining in the stricken vessel and yet, with no thought for his own safety, he devoted himself to the care of his injured comrades until such care was no longer required. His conduct throughout showed immense personal courage deserving of formal recognition. He acted in the highest tradition of the Royal Army Medical Corps.

Not for the first time had this country gone to war to defend a principle. It would not be the last. Nor would it be the last time that two brothers brought up overseas in colonial East Africa had found their way to serve this country by taking almost identical but separate paths in their pursuit of a career that they followed for the next twenty or so years.

This is the story of Pierre, the older brother, told by his younger brother Michael. They grew up in a family which was held in esteem until African politics intervened and South London found itself with another displaced family from Tanzania. When they grew old enough, both enlisted in the Royal Army Medical Corps. The work they did daily as trained professionals had its own element of magic in it, but its continuity became part of life's normality.

In Pierre's case, he was called upon to raise his game by way of duty to a level of commitment that almost defies rational explanation. Despite everything, what prevailed was his skill, driven by his humanity. He could not see his fellow men left in the conditions he was also experiencing. He had to try, for several hours, to the undying thanks of many soldiers, to salvage those damaged individuals on board the Sir Galahad, now a smoking wreck. He was one of the last to leave the vessel by helicopter, the piloting of which was itself a heroic act that day.

Pierre's heroism that day brought him the nation's gratitude in the form of the Military Medal. No one could doubt that he had earned it, yet he always felt that the Medical Corps ought to share it in some way; although it was his family who made him, it was those in the Corps who had shaped him to be able on that day to stand up and be counted. Pierre, this is your story.

CHAPTER ONE

Brothers in boyhood

Mzizima was the first recorded name of a small fishing village which developed into Dar es Salaam, now the capital city of Tanzania. Later the city was given the name Bander-as-salaam " meaning House of Peace" by the Sultan Seyyid Majid of Zanzibar. Over time the name evolved to Dar es Salaam meaning "Haven or Harbour of Peace", when it was colonised in the 19th century.

This is where five children were born to Rene and Rita Naya, two of them being the author and his elder brother Pierre.

From youthful escapades in the early 1960s to the later events of more than twenty years each in the Royal Army Medical Corps, the RAMC, this is our true story, with Pierre's experience of the Falklands campaign offered in his own words. I leave the reader to imagine how exceptionally proud I am of my beloved brother.

His personal descriptive accounts of that day and those that followed will be revealed in later chapters, and only then can you appreciate how and why he performed this heroic deed under the conditions of hostilities and war. He certainly had bottle. To even begin to understand how Pierre managed to cope with the pain, misery and death of his comrades on the 8th June 1982, you must understand his background. He was brought up by strict but loving parents with faith and trust in God and a natural ability to survive and do whatever is necessary in the hour of need. He was a born survivor. Such was Pierre's luck that we often teased him by saying that if ever he fell into a pile of manure, he would come out smelling like roses. Maybe it's the military humour.

Pierre was born on July 4th 1945. His full name was not Pierre but Peter Herlick Rene Naya. He got his German second name from the obstetrician delivering him, one of the doctors who had stayed on after the pre-colonial days in Dar es Salaam. Pierre was the nickname by which he was always known by everyone, throughout his life.

Pierre had his father's golden tanned skin, with black hair and brown eyes. He was of average height and stood at around 5 foot 8 inches tall, slimly built and very handsome indeed. He had immense charisma and personality and would entertain you for hours with his repertoire of music and jokes. He never appeared to lose his temper, even under duress. He had style. He was also a wonderful musician. Put a guitar in his hands and there was no stopping him.

He appeared always to have a cheeky grin and mischievous eyes and you often wondered what 'no good' he had been up to. Always impeccably dressed, he would look smart in any attire he chose to wear. He looked every inch an athlete and was a good swimmer.

Pierre's wide musical knowledge, which he had gathered so quickly, marked him out as a naturally gifted musician for whom playing to an audience provided a special thrill. Other rival players would try to emulate Pierre's mastery of keys and chords, but were never the same without his personality.

It was just one aspect of his developing character and charisma. Another was his ability to master repertoire quickly. He loved both the guitar and entertaining. He was a showman of immense talent, and could mimic all accents.

Pierre was a great communicator and storyteller, and somehow remembered countless jokes and ditties. He would be the life and soul of any party and would have you in stitches. He had a knack of mimicking anybody he wanted to. He had a great knowledge of accents and was extremely popular with people. He was in the Eric Morecambe mould for mimicking people.

As a musician in his teenage years, back in Dar es Salaam in the early 1960s, he developed a meaner and more aggressive stage manner. He rapidly began to emerge as a personality who became the hub of attention, with a developing fan club of young women. His military pals nicknamed him 'powerful Pierre' because of his very strong personality.

Our father, Jules Rene Naya, was born, one of a large family, on the main island of Mahe in the Seychelle Islands on the 27th April 1915. His whole family all emigrated from the Seychelles to Tanzania in search of work. Affectionately known by us all as Pop, he moved to Tanzania to improve his career prospects like the rest of the family. A very practical man in many ways, he was a motor mechanic by trade with a skill for brilliant innovation. His parents, by then, lived in the Arusha area of Tanzania, in the foothills of Mt Kilimanjaro.

Our father had the trade mark of a Naya, in that he was bald. All his brothers and my uncles had very distinctive baldness and receding hairlines, a trait which I and Pierre developed in later years. Pop, like Pierre, was tanned and of slim stature. Dad's father, our grandfather was born on the 16th June 1881 on the beautiful holiday paradise island of Praslin in the Seychelles, of Seychellois descendants.

Mother, Rita Solange Isnard, was born in Mombasa, Kenya on the 21st June 1926 to Seychellois parents. Mum was the youngest of three sisters. Our parents met in Dar es Salaam, when mother was a teenager.

Being Catholics, contraception was an issue, especially in those days. Mother, especially in her later years, could always be seen with her rosary in her hand at quiet moments, saying her daily prayers. She was married at the age of sixteen and had five children, four boys and a girl. They were, in order from the eldest, Robert Louis Rene, Peter (Pierre), then me, Michael Ronald Douglas, two years later, followed by Andrew Brian and then my only sister, Marianne Marion.

Pop was twenty-four years old when they got married, at St Joseph's Cathedral in Dar es Salaam. Neither Pop nor Mother had any formal education for any sustained period of time, but were both extremely hard working and made a joyous couple.

Mum was white-skinned with fair hair, very short, around five foot tall, and slim, even after giving birth to five children. She was often mistaken for a European lady, and had an abundance of energy and a real zest for life. Both our parents spoke English and French as well as Kiswahili, the local language, which we as teenagers all spoke. English was the spoken language of choice in our household.

The reader may have gathered from reading this far that our mother was a retiring wife and mother and very happy to be so. On reflection, while we were enjoying our collective youth and pursuing our interests, our mother was really the driving force of the family. She had a tremendous zest for life, a visionary imagination and, just like parents the world over, great resolve to improve all her children's prospects for the future and subsequent careers. She was a dynamo in our lives.

Mum owned a fairly large plot of land just outside the city. Her dream was to build a large family home there one day, when finances allowed. Every so often she felt the need to check on her plot and we would all go in Pop's car to view it. It was covered with scrub with a few coconut trees, and she would ask us to picture its development, describe exactly where the rooms would be and what shape and where the back yard would be. This was her vision for us, her family, sadly to remain unrealised.

As well as looking after a normal household with five children she also managed to hold down a job at Twiga Hotel on Acacia Avenue, now Samora Avenue in the city. It is no longer a hotel, but the building is still there with all the modern shops and a mall around it. As well as this job as a chambermaid she had a second job as the owner of a confectionery shop in the city centre, right opposite our favourite café, Cosy Café . She eventually sold this off to an uncle.

My grandmother, Mrs Mary Isnard, had three daughters, of which mother was the youngest. Grandmother Isnard, who was a self-taught midwife in the city, was very well known and greatly respected by all in the African and Indian community and was known as Mama Isnard.

At a time when seeking medical help was too expensive to be considered by the majority of the population, Grandmother Isnard filled the need for experienced help with childbirth. She would be called out at all times of day and night, taking her medical bag as people would call to collect her and stay away for hours at a time delivering babies and taking care of women's health. She charged nothing and worked in a spirit of charity, contributing her skills to help those vulnerable individuals with nothing to give.

She was always being greeted on the streets by people who wanted to show her the child she had brought into the world. This was adequate repayment for her charity, but everywhere she went she would be recognised. Food, drink and invitations to christening and birthday parties would be showered on her. I have since heard that Mama Rita, as she was often called, actually delivered George DeSouza, who was later to become the lead singer and bassist for Pierre's band, the Blue Shadows. Now residing in Canada, a professional musician and entertainer, he recalls my grandmother with fondness.

With her blonde hair and white skin, she resembled a European matriarch who spoke fluent Kiswahili, and she commanded great respect and authority wherever she went. Despite this, she was a very humble lady. I stayed and lived with my grandmother, and generally looked after her, for a few years, when she lived in her own large house in the city, on the corner of Arab Street. Grandma had a heart problem, palpitations as she recalls it, cardiac fibrillations. Being independent, she asked my mother if I could live with her and look after her. I often had to run to the local Indian doctor in town and ask him to come and see to her. God, it frightened me! This was my first life-changing experience in the caring profession which in later years became my career.

I must have been 14 years old then. I applaud and love her and remember her with much joy and admiration. Bless her. She sadly passed away while living in Australia in her later years, at the age of ninety. She is a hard act to follow.

Marianne, our only sister, resembled mother in many ways, being very blonde and fair-skinned with a lithe figure. Eldest brother Robert and youngest brother Andrew were also white skinned and took their hair colour from Mum's side, but saddled with the telltale trait of the Nayas' baldness and receding hairlines in later years.

We were all born at the Ocean Road Hospital in Dar, which, by the time we five arrived, was run jointly by British and German staff. This had been built during the time of the German administration. We all had second and third names, usually taking my father's name of Rene plus a second to commemorate the doctors or obstetricians looking after us at birth. Being Roman Catholic, we all had Christian names, but I'm sure Mum ran out of names to think of; hence all the English ones and in Pierre's second name of Herlick, a German name.

This magnificent hospital, which still stands today in all its glory, was built and completed by the Germans in 1897 and added to by the British. It has a beautiful Moorish, Germanic architectural style, typical of the buildings of that era. It overlooks the open, beautiful shores and beach of the Indian Ocean, just outside the harbour of Dar and not far from the State House. A beautiful location.

It is fringed by the feathery leaves of the mavinjee trees (casuarinas) which emit the lovely sound of the sea breeze, discarding their tiny prickly, marble-sized acorns all around the base of the tree.

The view across the wide warm ocean is punctuated by all the ocean-going ships waiting in turn to enter the harbour and discharge their loads. At sunset the spectacular yellow-orange glow of the African sun is breathtaking when seen across the shimmering and sparkling waves as it descends slowly into the sea in the distant horizon.

This seafront is a favoured spot for fruit and coconut sellers hawking their wares and overlooks the tiny uninhabited island of Bongoyo, some two miles away.

It is also a favourite spot at weekends for all the pretty Indian community girls to parade up and down this avenue dressed in their best regalia and finery. What a spot for talent spotting for us testosterone fuelled boys!

Many a day we spent in later years fishing and swimming in the warm waters of this seafront. To this day it brings back very happy memories whenever I visit the city. The hospital has marvellous distinctive twin-domed towers, topped by green iron spikes, very reminiscent of the German era in East Africa. It is still there in all its glory, now providing palliative care for the residents of Dar es Salaam.

Pop was a motor mechanic by trade. He worked throughout his life as one who knew the workings of any vehicle backwards. He had a great love for motor vehicles and there wasn't any problem or repair he could not solve. Because of his knowledge and ingenuity, he was widely respected in the community and in great demand as 'George', for most Africans could not pronounce his real name, Rene.

Despite, or perhaps because of, the influence of the motor car in our family, our mother never mastered driving one, which was quite puzzling to us boys as we thought it was the easiest thing to learn and do. Once or twice she would endeavour to get behind the steering wheel, with us boys taking it in turns to change the correct gear for her. I am sure she felt there was enough for her to do looking after five children.

At varying times, in the early days, and when pushed, mother did employ a local African man to help her in the household chores. He helped in every way, like washing, ironing, cleaning and odd jobs. He was regarded as part of the family. I remembered him by the name of Juma. His salary would have been in kind, like providing provisions and clothes. I recall, when we lived in bigger houses, with staff quarters attached, he would have his family also staying and being useful, especially with the chickens in the back yard and generally. He worked for us for a couple of years.

Tanzania has just about everything that Africa has to offer, be it tropical islands, climbing the highest mountain in Africa, Mount Kilimanjaro, diving or watching the annual migration of plains game in and around the Serengeti National Park. Long gone is the darker side of Dar es Salaam's history of slave trading and Tanzania is, without doubt one of the most exciting countries in the world and boasts some of the most romantic and tropical beaches in Africa. Zanzibar's Stone Town was once home to sultans and explorers and is the land of exotic, white, palm-fringed beaches, spices and azure waters.

Close your eyes and conjure up the quintessential image of Africa. The drama of the wildebeest migration along an infinite savannah. The incongruous snow cap of Mount Kilimanjaro and the proud tall, red-robed, and lanky Masai warriors stalking the plains, shepherding their herds of cattle and goats. Throngs of wildlife roam free in sprawling national parks and fishermen still plough the turquoise waters off Tanzania's coast in dhows.

Known as the Swahili Coast, Tanzania was a favoured stop on ancient trading routes between the Indian subcontinent and the

Middle East. Spices, jewels and slaves once passed through, bringing with them a melange of cultural riches that remain today.

The colourful language of Swahili, referred to as Kiswahili, was born here and features words not only of African origin, but ones from as far away as Indonesia and China. The ruins of once sophisticated cities with their old mosques, Arabian style, Germanic houses and coral palaces still remain, while places like Stone Town in Zanzibar and Bagamoyo on the mainland are still today living testaments to the Swahili coastal tradition that has gone on for thousands of years.

After the sultan's death in 1874 Dar es Salaam fell into decline. However in the 1880s, the arrival of German colonialists and Christian missionaries from many European countries coincided with the city's revival which led to its becoming the bustling commercial capital of Tanzania it remains. While the country changed its name, the capital city confidently retained its own, as it developed into its present position as the country's most important administration and commercial centre.

In a period of particularly rapid growth after WW2, Dar es Salaam put particular emphasis on developing services such as the transport network, health and water distribution.

In 1916, when it was part of German East Africa, Dar es Salaam was bombed and captured by the British. The magnificent state house along Ocean Road in the city was damaged severely and the German governor escaped to the Tabora region inland, which is virtually in the centre of the country. Under British control, it was renamed Tanganyika and retained this name even when it regained independence in December 1961, while choosing to remain under the umbrella of the Commonwealth. This critical transition to "Uhuru", meaning freedom, was achieved under the guidance of the first president, Dr Julius Nyerere, and it was only later that its name was changed to Tanzania, when Zanzibar, a tiny island off its eastern shore, merged with it in 1964.

Not without its benefits, the present Muslim president Jakaya Mrisho Kikwete, the fourth president, has been marred by widespread corruption, continuing an unfortunate tendency set in previous presidencies.

As a matter of personal interest, Zanzibar is commonly known as Freddie Mercury Island because it is the birthplace of the late lead singer of the rock band Queen. Born in September 1946, his real name was Farrokh Bulsara and he was a Parsi from the Gujarat region of India. At the age of 17, around the same time as Pierre and I, Mercury fled with his family from Zanzibar for safety reasons due to the 1964 Zanzibar Revolution in which thousands of Arabs and Indians were killed. His family, like mine, came to settle in England also in the same year.

Tanzania's political stability and geographical position continue to make Dar es Salaam an attractive choice for investment and today, with its vibrancy, attracts many foreigners and investors, from all parts of the world.

Julius Nyerere was responsible mainly for the country's transition to independence from British rule. The Roman Catholic son of a powerful Zamaki tribal chief, he taught history and biology at St Mary's Catholic Boys' School operated by the White Fathers. In 1949 he went to Edinburgh University, the first African to do so, and became president of the Tanzania African Association. He converted this into the political organization TANU, Tanzania African National Union. He continued in power until he resigned in 1985.

After independence there was pressure to replace Asians, Europeans and other ethnic minorities with Africans in all administrative and business sectors. This was one of the main contributing factors to our decision to leave Tanzania for UK.

There was an impatience at the slow pace of development and a tremendous demand for basic education and health services for the

African community. In reality, the Africans were not yet ready for self-rule. This became obvious years down the line.

President Nyerere made plans for a radical change and a programme of socialist development was introduced. This was based on self-reliance, broadly following the Chinese communist model. Many mistakes were made.

Despite the effects of the politicians, in the early years of independence, as I remember it, Dar still retained an enviable reputation for being a gloriously located city with a beautiful deep water natural harbour, parklands, cosmopolitan shops with acacia trees lining immaculately-kept avenues and a vibrant commercial centre.

For several years now I have made annual charity visits to Tanzania, working, teaching and mentoring in an upcountry hospital and its operating theatres. Passing through Dar es Salaam, I see the high-rise blocks, hotels and shopping malls of a major reconstruction programme. In exchange for Tanzania's rich minerals, mainly copper, the Chinese are involved in major road construction and building reformation on a very large and disturbing scale. Billions of dollars are given to the government, with hardly any signs of it trickling down to benefit the local population. Bribery and corruption operates on a major scale.

Despite these observations I am very proud of our birthplace and my country and their part in African development, while remaining an eclectic mix of Swahili, German, Asian and British peoples and architecture reflecting its colonial past and more recent history.

Tanzania contains three of Africa's best known lakes. Lake Victoria lies in the north, Lake Tanganyika of David Livingstone the explorer fame is in the west and Lake Nyasa lies in the south. There are numerous game reserves. Those in the Ngorongoro crater and the Serengeti are probably the most famous, but there are many others.

Large numbers of tourists are attracted to these areas from all over the world. But the grandfather to them all is the snow-capped Mount Kilimanjaro in the north of the country, which is the highest point on the African continent at 19,340 FT (5,895M). Its peak is named Uhuru, meaning freedom.

CHAPTER TWO

Go west, young man

The republic of Seychelles is an island country spanning an archipelago of some one hundred and fifteen islands in the Indian Ocean. Its capital, Victoria, on the largest island of Mahe is about 930 miles due east of the Tanzania port town of Tanga on the north east coast of Tanzania. Dar es Salaam, the capital of Tanzania, is 125 miles due south of Tanga. The island of Zanzibar lies about 50 miles off the East African coast with its capital, Zanzibar City, on its west coast facing Africa. I feel extremely proud to be able to say that the birthplace of our mother and Pop and their parents is this beautiful island paradise of the Seychelles.

Independence from Great Britain was granted in 1976. Nowhere else on earth will you find unique endemic specimens such as the fabulous coco-de-mer, the largest seed in the world, the jellyfish tree, with only eight surviving examples, the Seychelles paradise flycatcher and Seychelles warbler.

Seychelles is also home to two UNESCO World Heritage Sites, Aldabra, the world's largest raised coral atoll, and Praslin's Vallée de

13

Mai, once believed to be the original site of the Garden of Eden where the palm, the "Tree of Good and Evil" is to be found.

The legendary Vallée de Mai on Praslin is where the wondrously-shaped coco-de-mer nut grows high on ancient palms. This is the only place in the world where the fruit grows. Now nearly extinct, they require a special licence to be removed from the island. The tree grows to 25 metres tall. The leaves are fan-shaped, seven metres long and four metres wide, with a four-metre petiole.

Legend has it that sailors who first discovered the double coconut floating in the sea thought it resembled a woman's buttocks. This is reflected in its old botanical name *Lodoicea callipyge*, which roughly translates as "beautiful rump". The fruits of the Coco de Mer only grow on female trees, the male trees have long phallus shaped catkins, almost a metre long. Because of the erotic shapes, some say the trees make passionate love on stormy nights.

From the smallest frog to the heaviest land tortoise and the only flightless bird of the Indian Ocean, Seychelles nurtures an amazing array of endemic species within surrounds of exceptional natural beauty. Today, the 87,000-strong Seychellois population continues to reflect its multi-ethnic roots. Traditionally, the islands have attracted a broad diversity of people, from the four corners of the earth, including freed slaves, European settlers, political exiles, adventurers and traders of Arab and Persian origin as well as Chinese and Indians. Practically every nation on earth has been represented in this melting pot of cultures, each one contributing its special influence to today's vibrant yet tranquil society.

French Creole and English are widely spoken, and today the islands have a mixed population of British, Asians, Chinese, Arabic and other ethnic minority groups. Echoing the grand assortment of people who populate Seychelles, Creole cuisine features the subtleties and nuances of French cooking, the exoticism of Indian dishes and the piquant flavours of the Orient.

Grilled fish or octopus basted with a sauce of crushed chillies, ginger, and garlic are national favourites, as are a variety of delicious curries lovingly prepared with coconut milk, and innovative chatinis made from local fruits such as papaya and golden apple. As might be expected, seafood dishes feature predominantly in the local cuisine, appearing alongside the national staple, rice.

Seychelles, one of the world's very last frontiers, promises and provides adventure and breathtaking natural beauty in pristine surrounds which are still untouched by man.

Despite all the attractions of their home in the Seychelles, our grandparents on both sides of the family followed the adage, "Go west, young man" to reach the eastern seaboard of central Africa. Pop found work in Dar es Salaam and we were born and brought up there. All five children were educated at St Joseph's Roman Catholic School in the heart of the city centre. It sat next to the Gothic-style cathedral with its magnificent stained windows that had been constructed in 1897, taking five years to complete. It still retains all original details including the wooden confessional boxes and its magnificent organ. If ever you visit this city and are in the area, a visit to the cathedral is very worthwhile.

Both Pop and Mum were strong believers and Catholicism was their faith, so we were all baptised and confirmed as Catholics in this wonderful cathedral. For generations all our families and friends were Catholics. With this came the development of our social discipline, both behaviour and speech. Swearing and bad language, even as teenagers, were never tolerated. It was not even contemplated in our household unless you wanted to feel the weals inflicted by a caning from Pop's trouser belt.

We moved in a circle of Catholic friends and Pierre's strong faith permeates his descriptive personal accounts of that fateful day in 1982 in the Falklands, which called upon all his inner strength to cope with the trauma, as later narratives by Pierre describe that day in detail.

The cathedral and school command a fine view overlooking the harbour, jetty and ferry terminal. It was the main hub of activity in the city and from there it took some three hours by very modern catamarans for passengers to reach Zanzibar and outlying islands.

Our school buildings surrounded on three sides a large interior playing area. With temperatures in the yard easily reaching 30-40 °C, the large trees surrounding it provided much-needed shade in the heat of the day. Forming part of the yard was a magnificent and lovingly-tended garden, with many tropical plants and shrubs. We wouldn't dare pick a single flower petal, as this area was overlooked by all classrooms and teachers' rest rooms.

This area also had a bicycle shed. In addition to fulfilling its original purpose it was used in other ways, and what fun and games we had as boys with the pretty girls there. Sometimes we got caught, to be followed by a caning in the headmistress's office. This was Sister Jacinta's domain and was clearly visible across the yard from the bike shed. She used a wooden ruler to hit the palm of your outstretched hand, often missing as you quickly withdrew your hand at the last possible moment. This made her even angrier, but never deterred us from kissing the girls behind the bike shed. She was not in the least vindictive and I would sum her as very capable, realistic, fair and lovable.

We all remember this diminutive nun who came from Switzerland to bring a strictly-disciplined approach to her duties as headmistress, for which we developed a great respect that matured into fondness. She had taught and known all previous generations of the family, including our parents. She took care to know all her pupils, understand their backgrounds in detail and speak personally to all parents. The name of Sister Jacinta will never be forgotten. Everybody who ever went to that school remembers her to this day, as she also remembered all generations of parents, who she also taught. Her memory was faultless. A greatly respected and loved nun, she is now in her nineties and now lives in Baldegg Sisters' Nursing Home in Switzerland. Sadly I have just heard that she has peacefully passed away.

Most of the teachers and priests would occasionally come to our home for dinner and drinks. Many were fun people when not being teachers and we would all mix very easily. We were apt and earnest pupils with a thirst for education and we knew how to behave too, so we had no problems being pupils at school and more relaxed at home.

There were exceptions though. I particularly remember a very strict French lady whose task it was to teach us her native language in school, who often visited us at home. She perfected the art of twisting our ears if we got our vocabulary wrong. She thought that as our parents and relatives spoke good French at home, we should be perfect too. We made ourselves scarce when she appeared at home. Life was too exciting for us teenagers to be worried by this small detail.

Another teacher I disliked was an Indian who taught us mathematics. He was tall, lanky, skinny and ugly, very geeky looking. Most teachers have a quirk, and his was to look at his exercised biceps as though he was in the gymnasium after every time he wiped the blackboard clean. We smirked when he did this but, to his annoyance, he never worked out why.

The school catered for all levels of education up to school-leaving age, which was sixteen or seventeen at the time or when you had taken your final examinations. Its kindergarten was a small isolated hexagonal construction in the middle of the school yard and the remaining rooms for teaching, libraries and administration were, with the laboratory, in the surrounding buildings. As well as day pupils, the school also made provision for boarders. The primary school building on two floors was to the left of the school yard, while the secondary classes were across the yard to the right. The nuns' and boarders' accommodation was in the far end of the primary block. The priests were in the main block in the cathedral grounds.

Morning assembly consisted of prayers and hymn singing. Education then was to the Oxford and Cambridge accredited "O" levels. In my case, I was finally in the sixth form and about to sit my finals when the decision was taken to leave Dar for life in the UK. Pierre had already left for the UK a few months earlier and joined the British Army, thus commencing his illustrious military career.

School terms for us all were exciting times in our lives and lessons were not to be missed, other than for illness reasons, because we enjoyed learning and, of course, we had our strongly supportive family background. Our teachers consisted of European missionary nuns and priest, mainly from Germany and Switzerland, who remained and settled in Tanzania after colonial rule gave way to independence. They were complemented by highly educated and proficient Asians from the Indian subcontinent who had settled in Dar.

Our mixed classmates included Asians, Europeans, French and Italians. We still meet and keep in touch with many of them who, like us, now reside in the United Kingdom.

There were no African students, not because the school was discriminating in any way but because at that time, no Africans could afford to go to school. Our schooling was extremely hard for Pop and Mom to afford for the five of us. All books had to be bought. Neatly covered in brown paper, they were passed down the family line. How they managed to pay school fees and keep us five at school amazes me to this day. Average class size was in the region of 35 pupils, mixed with boys and girls. One moved up a class or form every year.

Our parents were certainly not well off by any means, but always, they somehow pulled out all the stops for our education and progress. Providing us with school uniforms was no mean feat annually, as we grew very fast. We were all dressed immaculately in khaki shorts and white shirts with the school emblem over the left shirt pocket and white socks and black shoes. Girls wore blue skirts, not too short, and white blouses.

English, of course, was the primary language spoken and taught at school. We also studied French, Swahili and Latin, so both Pierre and I, like the rest of the family, grew up to speak Swahili fluently. Individuals I meet on my travels back to Tanzania today are surprised when I talk to them freely in Swahili. They don't see me as a "mzungu", an Englishman. Pierre never lost his ability to fluently speak Swahili.

Religious studies were obviously very important in a religious school. We were all baptized, confirmed and brought up as Catholics. For church services and some lessons we were marched to the cathedral next door in single file. Students brought up in other denominations were encouraged to attend too, although the opportunity to meet and chat to the pretty girls was probably a greater attraction. The cathedral was, for us, very familiar territory and, as a family, we all attended holy mass on Sundays. It was also an occasion to meet our friends and other families.

Today, this school, which provided one of the pillars of our youthful lives still stands with its garden and bike shed, providing primary education to the children of Dar es Salaam. Writing about our school has prompted me to research some of my old classmates and I am delighted to confirm that I am now in contact with a few of them once again, fifty years on.

I reflect on what fun times these were for us and the happiest days of our lives. We spent hours either swimming, fishing in this area of the city or just generally people watching. The jetty went out into the sea some fifty metres and stood on concrete pillars which were festooned in coral of all sorts, shapes and sizes.

The tropical-coloured sea fish swam in abundance and could be drawn into a frenzy by the prospect of some bait. Today you see the same species in aquariums up and down the country. Trying to catch these small fish was an art to be perfected.

This area on Sundays offered the spectacle of everybody out for their Sunday stroll along the harbour front. All the Indian ladies in their colourful saris mingled with hawkers selling an abundance of local fruits, sweets, coconuts and mangoes, creating a very colourful scene. The area was always buzzing with life.

The smell of *nyama choma* or *mishikaki*, meat of all varieties grilled on skewers on hot burning charcoal, was so appealing, defying anybody not to purchase any. The thought of that sweet aroma of spices and meat combination makes me salivate. The smell of open-air fires and grilling methods pervaded everywhere.

Of course, as boys, this was the place to see the very attractive girls parading themselves in all their finery. Talent spotting was at the same time a serious business and a great source of amusement, to add to meeting with classmates and friends. With Pierre's good looks he won the girls, hands down.

Today as I revisit the city of Dar with its now high rise blocks, new hotels and shopping malls springing up all over the city, its roads are so jam-packed with vehicles and buses that the place comes to a halt. Some of this chaos is because traffic lights often don't work or appear to be set to create further chaos, especially when controlled by so called traffic cops. Among all this, I stop to admire the familiar haunts.

The Askari monument, which is the centre of the city, appears to be the worst place for traffic jams. I am baffled by the abundance of high-class flashy vehicles on show. Where does the average African get that sort of money from? The monument is the most iconic landmark in the city of Dar es salaam, at the junction of Samora and Maktaba street. It depicts an African Askari soldier figure in bronze with rifle in hand in a threatening gesture of defiance, pointing his rifle towards the harbour. Originally, the statue here was of the German explorer and soldier Herman von Wissman, who suppressed the coastal Arab Revolt in 1888-9. The first statue was demolished in 1916 when the British occupied Dar es Salaam.

The present bronze statue, of the Askari soldier, is in memory of all those African troops who died in WW1 and was dedicated to them at the unveiling in 1927. The statue was made by Morris Bronze Founders of Westminster in London.

Proceeding west from the Askari towards the harbour on the left is the New Africa Hotel, where the old Kaiserhof Hotel once stood. This hotel in the 60s had an outdoor terrace overlooking the Lutheran church and the sea front. Pop and friends, as well as us in our teens, frequented this hotel for evening drinks while listening to a band playing in the background. We would just sit and converse and watch the city life go by. Even today I still have to visit this hotel to sample the ice-cold Tusker beer, Pop's favourite, whenever I am in the city. The chilled glass, misty with condensation, reminds me of my Dad all those years ago.

Swimming with hippos

Pop worked as a mechanic, the only trade he ever knew, for the then internationally-famous vehicle builder Rootes Group, which held the franchise and was the main dealer for Tanzania. The distributor was founded and owned by the very distinctive and powerful dynasty known as The Karimjee Jivanjee family.

Pop's earnings at the beginning of his working life were not paid in cash but in kind. He told us once that he was given bags of rice, potatoes or soap powder instead of a monthly wage. This obviously changed as time went on when he gathered responsibilities and money was required for rents and such like.

He was a loyal worker for the Karimjee dynasty and he stayed with them throughout his working life in Dar es Salaam, finally progressing to be a much-respected foreman of the company.

The Karimjee family strongly supported the local community, by building and donating community schools and gymkhanas, founding many charitable trust funds like hospitals and medical institutes for the poor and ailing in the community. For their philanthropy and community work Sir Tayebali and Sir Yusufali Karimjee Jivanjees received knighthoods from the British government.

The origins of the company go back to 1825 when Mr Jivanjee Budhabhoy, a trader from Kutch Mandvi in India, came to East Africa and settled in Zanzibar, where he established a small trading firm that grew to become a considerable merchant empire. He was succeeded by three sons. In 1861 the brothers separated and Karimjee set up his own business, exporting commodities such as ivory, copra, groundnuts, cereals, beeswax, cloves and other spices from Zanzibar and the East African mainland to India.

The business was later handed over to his three grandsons, who managed it very successfully. By the time Karimjee died in 1898 the company had established trade connections with Europe.

In 1943 the Karimjee Jivanjee estate was formed and the turning point in the company's fortunes came when the company Karimjee Jivanjee & Co Ltd. moved its head office from Zanzibar to Dar es Salaam after forming the International Motor Mart and Karimjee Properties. In Pop's days with them they sold Hillman, Humber and Sunbeam cars, all imported from the UK.

Today this majestic building still stands between the old Germanic post office, which is over one hundred years old, and the Lutheran Church, overlooking the green lush botanical garden. It is still a motor car dealership and now the headquarters of Toyota Tanzania. To see this beautiful building when I travel to the city fills me with considerably emotion and pride. I can still vividly see Pop and his beloved Wolseley motor car driving through the side gates. We had great fun touring around the workshops with all the activity going on and were very proud that our father was the foreman in charge. Later on, I also found it to be a good spot to sit and reflect on my many memories of the place and days gone by.

As the company developed, Pop moved to the bigger lorry division on the main road to the international airport in what's known as the Pugu area of Dar. It was also in this vicinity, on the outskirts of the city, where a huge warehouse stood. Here to earn pocket money we assembled bicycles imported from China. These came in boxes with parts strewn all over the place. We had to work out where certain parts went, frames, chains, wheels, spokes, mudguards, and others. This was no problem, as we all had bikes and knew the workings. I seem to recall around 200 bicycles had to be assembled in a few days only.

The standard black bicycle in Africa was extremely durable and could carry very heavy loads with no sophisticated gears. Large sacks of coal, wood, mangoes, beds, anything that needed moving would be loaded onto this workhorse of bikes. Free wheel was the norm. What fun we had there during this period as teenagers.

Pop bought his green Wolseley four-door saloon from an English couple who had crashed it. It had beautiful green luxurious leather upholstery. He knew that he could restore it to its original condition given his skill and all the equipment, as well as labour, to his disposal. He had the panel beating and paint sprayers and other tools there too to utilise.

We would visit the workshop together to see how the renovation was getting on. What a marvellous job he did within a few weeks, and he made us all very proud to be able to ride in this almost new car. It was the envy of all his friends, and ours too.

As he worked in this very large gated compound with askaris to watch over the area day and night, he decided to keep turkeys and more chickens. Imagine the sight of these birds roaming around among large lorries and equipment. It made us all laugh. He was a man with ingenuity and never missed a trick. A born survivor and our father too, with natural instincts. We were very proud of him.

A second idea took root because of the piles of wooden crates in which lorry spare parts were sent from the UK. He had at his disposal a large array of sturdy wooden planks of all sizes, lengths and widths, so instead of burning or disposing of such valuable material, he decided to build a fishing boat in our back yard.

The first boat was a prototype model to find out all the construction problems and resolve them. His idea was to build a larger boat with a small cabin to protect those on board from the searing heat of the sun.

As a family unit growing up in such a wonderful climate and idyllic country, we developed a love of fishing and the sea which was instilled by our father. As well as satisfying Pop's great interest in fishing, his idea was to bring home the catch of the day to support his growing family.

In Pierre's case this interest developed into a passion for fishing, boats and the sea that stayed with him throughout his life. He also gained a reputation for being a lucky fisherman and very often made the first and largest catch.

The second model was in the region of fifteen feet long with chines and a keel and ribs to provide support and shape to the packing case planks which were cut and shaped and then clamped in place. It had streamlined features which allowed the boat to cut through the seas with ease. To stop any leakage, Pop would caulk in between the planks, held tight by screws, with cotton sisal ropes or strings impregnated with tar. We would often help him build this boat and all his orders were dutifully carried out by us boys with no questions asked. We were never in doubt as to the success of his project.

He named our second boat *Souflette* and it could seat eight people on three rows of benches. We would often help him build this boat and admire his skills and improvisation. He eventually sold it, at great profit I am sure, to an Arab fisherman living and fishing off the historic town of Bagamoyo some miles along the northern coast of Dar es Salaam.

Our boat building project took place when we were living in a very upmarket residential area of Upanga, within easy walking distance of the sea and beach area. I remember this house as rather large with a flat roof terrace, which we often slept on to escape the heat of the night. There was no air conditioning in those days and the evening breeze gave immense relief. It also had a very large mango tree at the back that overlapped the terrace, providing it with much needed shade, as well as rich pickings in the mango season. This made it an ideal place for house parties and playing music.

Today, this is a diplomatic area with many embassy buildings. However, our old house still stands there after all these years. Whenever I am driven near there, I cannot resist asking the driver to slow down as I pass our house, just to bring back memories of happy times.

Before we had our boat, our only fishing was from the shoreline and rocks. It was all done with hand-held nylon lines. We did not possess any rods or reels, as these were very expensive and, in fact, unobtainable in any Dar es Salaam shops in Dar at that time. If we tried to fish at night, it could only be by moonlight, as we had no lights or lighting.

The narrow channel at the entrance of the harbour was one of Pop's favourite fishing sites. This area had a sandy beach, with a coral shelf some fifty metres out forming a step to the very deep water of the navigational channel from the Indian Ocean. This channel had to be deep enough to allow large ships to enter the harbour. Some large species of fish were caught here.

Without rods, we cast the nylon line with heavy weights at one end, swirling it around our heads faster and faster, just like a hammer thrower in athletics and then casting the line to the exact desired spot. It was a real art.

Along the Oyster bay area, as it's known, was another favourite fishing spot. It was close to the plush residences and diplomatic houses high up on the rocks that overlooked the crashing waves some thirty metres below. At least here you need not get your feet wet. Pulling up our catch was a tricky business, trying to prevent the fishing line being cut by the jagged sharp rocks below us. We always expected to lose many fish because of the extreme height we had to manoeuvre our catch to.

Pop knew all the best fishing spots in the beautiful harbour as well as the open sea, and many more would be found when we started to explore previously unvisited sites with our new boat. Pop moored *Souflette* just next to the now defunct Dar es Salaam Yacht Club within the harbour's perimeter. It was safe enough there, but he normally gave the night watchman a few shillings to keep an eye on it day and night.

At first, we did not own an outboard engine, so boy-power was needed to row the boat across to the designated fishing spot. This was extremely hard work, especially when the sea currents were against you. Many times we would come back from a fishing trip with blisters on both hands, yet had to be ready for school the following morning. I can't be certain that we never moaned at these privations, but we would always look forward to the next trip.

Eventually, Pop bought a second-hand outboard Seagull 5HP two stroke engine for our boat. This had a modified propeller shaft which he made in his workshops, to enable the small propeller blades to reach deeper into the sea water. This gave us much more speed and propulsion and duration. With it too, our blisters receded into the distant past. Pop would take and memorise the necessary bearings of landmarks and buoys for him to navigate us to wherever he had decided to fish. When these landmarks, usually the church steeple or tall building, lighthouse or buoys, came into line with another mark we would drop anchor and catch our breath and relax momentarily. Pop was very fussy and even if we were only slightly off the desired spot, he would ask us to move again.

He was canny too and sometimes, if other fisherman were in the same area and watching us, he would decide not to go straight to his location but would fish just nearby until the coast was clear. He fearlessly guarded his current favourite spot, which might be the site of an old wreck which could provide very good fishing.

There was always a big element of chance about fishing. If it was with you on the day, our mother could be relied upon to turn the catch into something delicious for our next meal.

Fishing over an old wreck was very rewarding. All fish caught were destined for the pot and nothing was wasted. We would often descale and gut our fish while still out at sea. Fishing was also about being lucky on the day. Pierre was a lucky fisherman and very often caught the first one. His love of fishing was born and nurtured in this environment. Pierre's knowledge of rods, lines, reels and knots of every description developed and became, in time, encyclopaedic to a degree unrivalled by his peers. So much so that he achieved his skipper's licence after sitting many exams in navigational skills for small fishing boats. Much later, he owned his very own luxury high-powered deep sea fishing vessel in the Portuguese Algarve, where he lived.

The *Souflette* opened up further locations and fishing spots and also allowed us to outrun the local Africans to the better spots. African fishermen used the *ngarawas*, a handmade boat carved from one large piece of tree trunk, usually from the mango tree. This was hollowed out with precision using a hand chisel and hammer.

No electrical equipment such as drills was ever used in manufacturing these hand-crafted vessels. Strong ropes attached side balusters to one side of the boat like outriggers, for extra stability. Some also had a makeshift sail, made from any material available like large sheets or tarpaulins. These boats were very sleek and cut through the waves with ease and cover great distances. They were normally crewed by two persons maximum, as space was of premium. We could outrun them, however, with our Seagull power, so the race was on. They were fun times, racing the locals, taking it in turns at the helm of the boat, dodging the driftwood and riding the bigger waves. We were quickly learning the ways of the sea.

Handline fishing needed a lot of concentration, discipline and patience. The line is held taut, resting on the index finger of the right hand, with the thumb of the same hand very lightly securing the line. When the fish takes the bait, the tug-tug sensation is felt by the index finger, when at the same precise time you have to strike or yank sharply, thus allowing the hook to be engaged in the jaws of the fish.

The bigger the fish, the harder the tug. Curling or resting the nylon line around toes was a cardinal sin and discouraged for obvious reasons.

Usually the fishing day started with a visit to the local market, to buy our bait for the day's trip. Pop would choose a couple of kilos of the most succulent large prawns available. These prawns were larger than the average size of an index finger, but they were cheap and plentiful.

Young small squids or baby octopus were also choice bait. The fish appeared to be choosy and we found that they liked certain baits at certain locations and times of the day. Juicy large oranges were our own preferred treat. Boat discipline was very important and everyone knew the drill, so lines would not become tangled and time wasted. All lines were folded neatly at your feet and not flung about.

Everyone knew where to sit to balance *Souflette* so she would not roll around unnecessarily. Movement was kept to the minimum. If the day's catch was abysmal and we had not used much of the bait, mother would make a delicious stir fry from the remaining large prawns and squids when we got back home.

In the far distance of the harbour, the sea formed an inlet of water resembling a creek area with mangrove plantation. This area was known as Kurasini and we lived in this very peaceful patch for a time. The sea and creeks, of course, were only walking distance from our house with its large backyard where, naturally, we kept chickens and turkeys.

In this area of the sea, large, delicious edible crabs and lobsters thrived. Catching crabs was a night-time experience which we all looked forward to with great anticipation and eagerness. Frankie, an older cousin of the family, encouraged this nocturnal activity. Frankie was the youngest son of my uncle, also named Frankie. He was completely bald and had once served in the King's African Army. This was not his choice, but he had been conscripted into the local army. He was also a motor mechanic for a Fiat company in the city. He was completely white-skinned with bright blue-green eyes and very bandy legs, all of which, with his natural exuberance, made him quite a character. He could easily pass as a 'Mzungu'.

Frankie lived with us, and consequently we took every opportunity to pursue these crustaceans with him. His contribution to our fishing technology was to weld together several large torches to make a very long, extremely powerful one, about two to three feet, that was so bright it could blind a rabbit at a hundred paces. It took countless batteries to power this huge torch, but it proved very effective on hunting expeditions.

He also made a harpoon out of a steel rod, with tiny barbs at the end. This also proved itself when we went crab hunting.

Walking at night into the mangrove area, waist high in the warm, calm sea water, shining the torch's beam into the clear waters encouraged these inquisitive creatures to investigate right up to our exposed feet, which made our toes very vulnerable. The powerful beam of light would hypnotise the crab momentarily for long enough for it be harpooned. A night's catch would produce up to twenty or so crabs. These would be put into hessian bags and quickly taken home to be dumped into boiling water alive, with a heavy weight on the lid.

Occasionally we did have dramas when some tried to escape. That was the final excitement of the whole crabbing trip. A bitten toe was a frequent consequence of our crabbing nights, but Mother's delicious curries more than made up for the pain.

This particular creek with its sandy beach and coconut trees on the shoreline was also the home of a pod of hippos. Hippos also have the name of 'Satan's pigs'. Many a night we would disturb their peace and hear their splashes in and out of the water some yards away, as one of us always kept a wary eye on their whereabouts.

They certainly did not distract us from our night's crabbing. We were either fearless or plain stupid. In the daytime this area was our favourite spot for swimming and fishing, jumping off rocks and diving from the home-made diving platform. This we built out of 44-gallon drums, four of them lashed together with ropes and attached to planks, which made a platform from which to dive off. We moored our platform some fifty metres from the shoreline.

Swimming across the half-mile estuary was no problem or concern to us boys, even with the hippos around. Nor did the width of Dar es Salaam harbour, with its variety of larger seagoing vessels to be dodged. As fit and energetic teenagers, the outdoor lifestyle suited us to a tee and this played a major role in our lives while living in Tanzania in the 60s.

We developed natural skills to go foraging in the countryside, where there was an abundance of edible things to be had. We never went hungry, as mangoes, papayas, coconuts, guavas, cassava, cashew nuts, water melons, bananas and oranges, just to name a few, were growing all around.

Shimming up a tall coconut tree, some thirty metres high, to get the very young nuts, full of their sweet milky water, was an easy feat for us. We copied the technique used by the local Africans. It involved a piece of rope tied in the figure of eight around our ankles, which gave enough grip to push up the tree trunk with arms wrapped around it. The locals carved footholds all the way up on some trees, which made them a doddle to climb.

The pawpaw or papaya fruit grew mostly wild in the fields and countryside. They were very large fruit and very tasty too. The tree can grow up to twenty metres or so, with enormous hand-shaped leaves which are often in tatters in appearance because of the wind. The trunk itself is very thin and could not take a man's weight climbing it, so harvesting pawpaw was a boy's job. But there are shorter varieties if searched for. The bunches of sweet fruit, only borne by the female tree, hang close to the trunk just below the leaves.

The local Africans do not regard the papaya as a commodity as it is so widely available in the wild. Its branches have other uses too. As youngsters we use to hollow out long sections to make a blowpipe, shooting out small stones or peas. A variation of this was to cut serrations into it along its length to make a musical flute.

All along vast areas, especially inland, you will see to this day many coconut trees with just their bare trunks and no tops at all. This saddens me a great deal as the locals "bleed the hearts of the tree" by lacerating its tender top parts and tying plastic bottles to catch the juices which flow out. They use it to ferment into alcohol.

The damage caused by this despicable and thoughtless action kills the tree, which eventually falls down and dies. It has become a sad story of wanton destruction.

Mango trees, or *embe* in Swahili, grow everywhere in Tanzania to a height of forty feet. They have a dense canopy of branches and leaves that create an ideal resting place for the locals and animals shaded from the heat of the sun. There are many varieties, but of course the best of all is the *embe dodo* or very large mango, about the size of an average outstretched hand and occasionally bigger.

The mango season occurs at the hottest time of year, December to February, but varies with other locations in the country. Mango fruit grow in bunches on long stalks some six inches long, dangling from all branches of this magnificent much-loved tree. To get the fruit down we would resort to throwing large sticks or stones, to bring down a bunch of mangoes at a time. This action caused the ripe mangoes to hit the hard ground with such a thud that the fruit would burst open to reveal the lovely juicy flesh, wasting half, if not most, of the delicious fruit.

Very early in our development as fledgling hunter-gatherers we had to master the art of making our own catapults. First find a 'Y' shaped branch which is strong enough to take the strain of serious use. Then all we needed was a discarded inner tube from a bicycle, from which we could cut the strips of rubber to provide the power. Narrower strips of rubber provided the lashings and an old leather boot was ideal for making into the pouch to hold the stone, or whatever you proposed to let fly with. The whole idea was to gather food for the family, but while being fairly powerful and accurate in skilled hands, these homemade catapults were really only of use when the prey remained still. However we did, as boys do, try to hit moving targets too.

Hanging fruit high above was ideal, especially mangos, but large tasty wood pigeons were easy prey, as were rabbits, which we could hit up to twenty-five feet away. However, we didn't have it all our own way. Lurking in the undergrowth and acutely sensitive to our presence were snakes. We were fearless, but also very careful. Many people die each year from snake bites, some very quickly. Snakes bites can kill you instantly, especially the highly venomous varieties, usually brightly coloured, although the black mamba is the most deadly snake commonly seen in the undergrowth we frequented. Snakes can hear you coming through ground vibrations created by footfall. They sense impending danger and most, but not all, will glide away from trouble.

However some snakes are arboreal, so we had to be on the watch out for them too. It meant that, much like an aircraft pilot, we had to be aware of our surroundings all the time, through 360 degrees.

The art of collecting mangoes was not to hit the actual fruit, but the long stalks holding the dangling bunches. Pierre in particular was a good shot. As he took aim, we would wait under the bunch for any dislodged mangoes and catch them before they hit the ground. He had to have a good aim, and we had to be good catchers. Our ammunition was either small stones or smooth sea pebbles, but for the best accuracy and speed, there was nothing better than old scratched and chipped marbles. We would start our expeditions with pockets bulging with stones and marbles and return home bulging with mangoes. At least, that was the plan.

We became very successful working as a team. Practice makes perfect, and by the time we were in our teens, we were also adept at making simple traps out of a length of string, a box and a small piece of wood. They were simple and effective- all we needed was patience.

Catching a rabbit would give us a great thrill and excitement, after stalking our prey for what seemed hours. To our list of potential prey we added love birds, our name for the plentiful, beautifully-coloured, very noisy parakeets, which had very sharp beaks.

The early morning sounds of the cockerels crowing in our back yard, and those of neighbours' too, were something I will never forget. The songs of the singing birds were a tonic to the ears, especially the great tits, black birds and sparrows. Who needs an alarm clock with the sound of the cockerels to wake you up?

However, at night-time it's a different story, as the African night sounds of the crickets and other insects can be deafening.

As a family growing up in Dar es Salaam, we all, at different times, suffered from malaria. It is not a pleasant disease. Caused by the bite of the Anopheles mosquito, it produces an incapacitating fever, with high body temperature, rigors and severe coldness, and shivering for a day or so. To this day I can never be a blood donor, as the disease stays in the bloodstream for years. We never slept under mosquito nets, although now, on my travels back to the Tanga region, I always make sure I use them in my hostel accommodation.

Malaria is a major public health problem in Tanzania and its annual death toll is estimated to be 60,000, with 80 percent of these deaths among children under five years of age.

Approximately 14 to 18 million clinical malaria cases are reported annually by public health services and more than 40 percent of all outpatient visits are attributed to it. Prophylactic treatment is the best answer today, so whenever I return to the country, I take Doxycycline tablets, prior to arriving in Tanzania and for the duration of my visit, then continue for the next four weeks.

The first cases of HIV/AIDS in Tanzania were reported in 1983, although, for sub Saharan Africa as a whole, the problem began to surface in the late 1970s. The epidemic has evolved from being a rare new disease to a common household problem, one which has affected most Tanzanian families. The development of the HIV/AIDS epidemic has had its clear impact on all sectors of development, not only the direct pressure on AIDS cases and management of resources, but through economic deterioration and debilitation of the active population, especially young men and women aged between fifteen and forty-five. HIV infection is unevenly distributed across geographic area, gender, age groups and social economic classes in the country. The percentage of the population infected by HIV ranges from less than three percent across most of the country to more than forty-five percent in certain sub-populations.

CHAPTER FOUR

Hunting adventures

Our cousin Frankie possessed a .22 calibre rifle. This opened up the possibility of hunting larger prey like bush bucks, small deer, antelope and the occasional wild boar. The countryside surrounding Dar es Salaam and beyond provided wild game in abundance, and hunting for our larder was a way of life.

In the Naya household there was always an air of excitement and anticipation when we were organising a hunting trip, as there were lots of hungry mouths to feed then. Many of our trips were at night and we would hunt until the early hours of dawn. In daylight we had to stalk our prey, which would give us one opportunity to make the kill. Sharp eyes, silence, concentration and acute hearing played a major part in achieving our goal.

All kills would be skinned, gutted and washed by us boys and barbecued over open log fires. Despite having no idea of the final game meat on the menu when we went on a hunt, we rarely failed to bring home some delicious meat. The sisal plantations around Dar were a good hunting ground concealing a wide variety of game, with the added attraction of being within reach of home.

At night we used the headlights of Pop's car or our bright and more effective spotlight mounted on the car's windscreen, which would sweep through 180° to illuminate any creature up to fifty metres. On occasion we would sit on the car's mudguards and bonnet, tapping lightly on the windscreen to guide the driver when we spotted anything. Once caught in the beam, the light reflected from the animal's eyes would give its position away and, for a very short time, it would appear to be mesmerised by the light, giving us a brief period to make our kill.

I remember one particular trip in Pop's Wolseley. Its green colour provided us with good camouflage as we drove for what seemed hours in an area we had not visited before. Pop must have heard of this spot from workmates or relatives, as we hardly saw any locals, even though this was a daytime trip.

The road was really a rough track, unpleasantly dusty with large potholes bouncing us around, with the sun pounding down on us adding to our discomfort. The familiar loud and distinctive noise of the African beetles and crickets broke up the bush silence.

Just off the road we spotted a fairly large gazelle some fifty metres or so in the light savannah grass, taking refuge and shade from an overhanging bush. Pop stopped the car very quietly and out came Frankie and Pierre, standing by the car taking aim. Bang! Frankie fired a single shot. Usually he fired off several shots automatically in his eagerness. Although this time, he managed to restrain himself. Wild birds flew off in different directions, disturbed, confused and frightened by the noise of the bang.

Telltale signs told us immediately that he had indeed hit the target. This was not often the case as, in my view, Frankie was not a good marksman, an opinion that would be, I am sure, supported by Pop and my brothers, including Pierre.

The trouble was that Frankie was the eldest in our group and the rifle belonged to him, so he got to take the shots. On this occasion he 'got lucky' and did hit the target, as we all saw the gazelle jump in the air, land and start to lamely run away. Today, I feel sure the animal welfare group would not approve of our tactics.

Bringing down a fairly large gazelle is a not a foregone conclusion. The shot needs to be placed either just behind the forelegs where the heart is, or a direct hit on the smaller and more difficult target of the head. On many occasions the animal, although hit, will run for a while before collapsing. This honed our skills for reading trails.

So off went Pierre and Frankie with rifle in hand into the bush in pursuit of this gazelle. After a few minutes they disappeared from sight, while the rest of us stayed near the car, trying to catch a cooling breath of wind.

After some fifteen minutes or so, we saw the dust trail of a vehicle approaching us in the distance. With horror, as the vehicle approached us, we immediately recognised it to be a game warden's distinctively coloured Land Rover, with its inscriptions on the side. In our wanderings that day we had ventured unintentionally into a game reserve. Pop would never venture on our hunting trips into game reserves, as they were definitely off limits, no matter how desperate we were for some game meat.

Pop muttered to us to remain calm and pretend nonchalantly to act as though we were refuelling our car from a jerry can he always carried in the boot. Travelling for miles in this terrain, there were no petrol stations and the worst scenario was to run out of fuel in the bush somewhere, miles from any habitation.

The two African game wardens, obviously looking to apprehend game poachers, must have heard the initial shot of the .22 calibre rifle and decided to investigate. Sounds in the stillness and heat of the day could travel for miles in this environment.

They approached us very, very slowly and suspiciously, and saw us waving and greeting them with big grins with the customary "jambo, habari", which is "hello, how are you?" They waved back at us and fortunately decided not to stop to ask any questions. Our charade worked and they did not think for a minute that the sound of the shot came from our party. We obviously looked too innocent.

Pierre and Frankie, who, apparently could see all this happening, immediately recognised who the men were and hid low in the undergrowth. Realising we could all be in severe trouble if caught, we watched the wardens continue very slowly down the road, until they were out of sight in the bend of the road. Pop, meanwhile, was gesticulating frantically towards where he thought Pierre and Frankie might be for them to remain low in the bush.

Without Pierre and Frankie, we then started to drive off very slowly in the direction of the wardens' Land Rover, but we never came across them. Pop continued down the road for almost an hour before deciding that the coast would now be clear. He turned round and retraced his tracks to pick up Pierre and Frankie.

Eventually, as we came round a bend in the road, we could see two figures limping towards us. We immediately thought that they had been injured. But as we drew closer, we could see it was Pierre and Frankie with the customary wide grin on Pierre's face. They had used their heads and decided to dismantle and hide the rifle by stuffing the various parts down their trouser legs. That was a clear case of thinking on their feet. Both were glad to get into the car, as they had been walking for some distance in the heat, and were extremely thirsty.

They didn't think for a minute that we had abandoned them in the bush in a remote part of the country. However, for all the action, we had no reward, as they had not found the injured gazelle. It was a disappointing end.

Our stamina and fitness as teenagers knew no bounds. We enjoyed cycling and were good cyclists. We would not think twice about a group of eight or nine of us leaving late in the coolness of the night to cycle, as a pack, one hundred miles away to the next town called Morogoro through wild countryside. We would arrive the following evening and sleep the night in the missionary hostel for free, high in the surrounding cooler hills. We would have then, have to return back to Dar es Salaam ready for school on Monday morning. Among our peers we were regarded as unique having done this memorable journey. No one else tried to emulate our trip.

Luckily for us this journey was by then on tarmac roads. We couldn't have done it on muddy and dirt tracks. The trip took us through wild country with the chance of sighting lions basking in the shade of the mango trees.

We were either extremely brave or downright stupid, or plain adventurous, to contemplate such a trip on bicycles with only small torches as headlights. Fearless is the word I would use to describe our actions. This was all on standard Raleigh bikes with no sophisticated gears or multi flywheels. The bikes were fairly heavy. I wonder how much further we would have got with today's very modern racers.

Little did I know it at that time, but I was to make numerous journeys by local bus along this same very road, fifty years on. The landscape has changed with more dwellings, but familiar features remain to remind me of that memorable time in our lives.

Of beer and bees

To see his mother, Pop had to drive Mum and the family to the region of Arusha, which lies in the foothills of Mount Kilimanjaro in the north of the country. The weather in this area was much cooler than the coastal city of Dar es Salaam. Arusha was the starting point for many tourists intending to visit the large, well-publicised game reserves of the Ngorongoro crater and Serengeti National Park.

Visiting any of the parks, especially Serengeti, you would expect to see some of the millions of wildebeest, each one driven by the same ancient rhythm of life. Instinct drives each animal round its inescapable cycle of life involving a frenzied three-week bout of territorial conquests and mating, when it is survival of the fittest as 25-mile columns plunge through crocodile-infested waters on the annual exodus north to find fresh grazing. There they replenish the species in a brief population explosion that produces more than 8,000 calves daily before the 600-mile return migration begins again through the same hazards.

Tanzania's oldest and most popular national park is also a world heritage site and recently proclaimed a seventh worldwide wonder.

The Serengeti is famed for its annual migration, when some six million hooves pound the open plains, as more than 200,000 zebras and 300,000 Thomson's gazelles join the wildebeest's trek.

Yet even when the migration has taken these animals far to the north, the Serengeti offers arguably the most scintillating game viewing in Africa. Here great herds of buffalo remain with smaller groups of elephants and giraffes and thousands of eland, topi, kongoni, impala and Grant's gazelle to be seen.

The spectacle of predator versus prey dominates Tanzania's greatest park. Golden-maned lion prides feast on the abundance of plain grazers. Solitary leopards hunt the acacia trees lining the Seronera River, while a high density of cheetahs prowls the south eastern plains.

Almost uniquely, all three African jackal species occur here, living alongside the spotted hyena and a host of more elusive small predators, ranging from the insectivorous aardwolf to the beautiful serval cat. But there is more to Serengeti than large mammals. Gaudy agama lizards and rock hyraxes scuffle around the surfaces of the park's isolated granite koppies. A full one hundred varieties of dung beetle have been recorded.

There are over five hundred bird species, some even migrating annually to Europe. They range from the outsized ostrich and the bizarre secretary bird of the open grassland to the black eagles that soar effortlessly above the Lobo Hills.

Enthralling as the game viewing is, the immediate effect on the visitor is a liberating sense of space that the Serengeti Plains bring, stretching across sunburnt savannah to a shimmering golden horizon at the end of the earth.

Yet, after the rains, which come around April each year, this golden expanse of grass is transformed into an endless green carpet flecked with wild flowers. There are also wooded hills and towering termite mounds, rivers lined with fig trees and acacia woodland stained orange by the dust.

Popular the Serengeti might be, but it remains so vast that you must take care, should you be the only human audience when a pride of lions masterminds a siege, focused unswervingly on its next meal. All this was in our back yard, so to speak.

This three-day journey to Arusha in the north would take Pop through Tanga in the northern part of the country, along unmade roads and rutted dirt tracks made worse by potholes and mud during the rainy seasons when the roads could be washed away and all but impassable except by 4x4 vehicles. That is hard physical driving while trying to avoid upsetting the wildlife. Lions and elephants are not to be pushed around. This, indeed, was real safari country in the 1960s. Today the modern touristy safari and game reserves do not appeal one bit to me, as we had seen the real safari in our teens.

Today, the same journey would take six to eight hours in buses driven crazily fast over only slightly better roads. I experience this each year, because I travel to Tanzania to help for about a month in the operating theatres of a hospital not too far from Tanga, so the journey from the airport in Dar es Salaam takes me over these same roads.

Whenever the opportunity arose and the conditions allowed, Pop would encourage us to develop our driving skills. He was an excellent teacher. We never had a single driving lesson from anyone else, but we all passed our driving tests first time. Having driving assistants allowed Pop to rest more often on the journey, sometimes encouraged by a bottle of Tusker. It has become my favourite beer too, and whenever I am in Dar, I make sure I don't leave without confirming that its quality is being maintained.

With its climate, Dar has a wide range of good local beers to offer. As well as Tusker these include Kilimanjaro, Serengeti, Ndovu and Safari. Often, straight after a fishing or shooting trip, we would go to the Splendid Hotel for drinks. All beers sold were of the bottled variety. Out came the waiter bringing, on Pop's instructions, Cokes or ice creams for us. Occasionally we all went into the bar area, just sitting and chatting or playing cards.

Mother and Father made a very sociable couple. Life went on at a gentle pace, with great good humour. Meeting up with other relatives and friends was always the highlight of an evening.

Evening trips would include going to the Indian sector of town, where the speciality would include *nyama choma* or skewered grilled meat or *mshikaki* cooked on open coal fires just outside the restaurant door. The sweet, spicy, aroma would fill the air and get the taste buds flowing. This was served with a sweet and sour source made out of tamarinds. Finger-licking stuff. Curries of all different types and styles were to die for.

Dar es Salaam cuisine was a fantastic mixture of different cultures such as Indian, Goan, Chinese, Arabic, Swahili and English. Mum was the master of all these dishes and we would watch and observe her culinary skills. Pierre could make a mean curry. All this rubbed off on us. In later life he baked and beautifully decorated cakes of all shapes and sizes exquisitely. In his drive to improve his skills he took a cake-decorating course, finding himself the only man among all the women at the night school he attended, and of course outshining all of them.

Vegetables, meat and spices of all varieties and tastes were readily available and cheap to buy. Indian cuisine is characterised by a great variety of foods, spices, and cooking techniques. The most important spices in this type of cooking are chilli pepper, black mustard seed, cumin, turmeric, fenugreek, ginger, coriander and asafoetida (hing). Another very important spice is garam masala, which is usually a powder of five or more dried spices, the most common being cinnamon, cardamom and clove.

Leaves like bay leaf, coriander leaf, mint leaf and curry leaves are commonly used. This use of curry leaves is typical of Indian Creole cuisine. In sweet dishes, cardamon, cinnamon, nutmeg, saffron and rose petal essence are used. Zanzibar is the main provider of these spices, which gave rise to its common name of The Spice Island.

Opposite the old yacht club once stood the Dar es Salaam Club, which was much frequented by Europeans, business people and diplomatic staff. It was a magnificent building in the old colonial Germanic style. It appeared to me that there was always something sparkling and attractive happening there, like dances accompanied by live music. In direct contrast today, sadly, it is a government building and has lost all its old vibrancy.

Past Ocean Road hospital is the famous Gymkhana Club, which still provides facilities for many sports like football and hockey, and the only golf course in Dar es Salaam, which meanders through leafy avenues in sight of the ocean.

Further along Ocean Road is another landmark called Selander Bridge, which connects the peninsula to the city boundaries. This area, known as Upanga, is where we once lived. To the right of Selander Bridge, another facility provided by the Germans is the lovely pristine sandbank and beach from which Pierre, I and the rest of the family learnt to swim. This sandbank and beach is still visible today and a tear fills my eye every time I pass. Nearby, a new American Embassy stands - the previous one was bombed during a terrorist attack a decade ago. The new embassy is huge, with all underground services and tight security.

Further on still is Oyster Bay, with its beautiful Kunduchi and Silver Sands holiday resorts, with white sandy beaches and a backdrop of splendid new hotels. This is also the main European residential area of Dar. Most diplomatic staff are housed here too.

Another long stretch of golden sands and crystal-clear waters, fringed with coconut and palm trees, is known as Coco beach and is a fantastic spot for swimming, sunbathing and people watching. Today it has been developed to provide a mix of housing, bars, restaurants and shops.

Towards the northern end of the beach lie some rocks. I remember them very well, as one day in our youth, Pierre nearly drowned here. He and cousin Frankie were up on the rocks above the sea below looking for a likely spot to dive from, when they disturbed some bees. Swarms of angry African bees react badly so, to evade them, Pierre and Frankie's only option was to dive into the sea. The rocks were some twenty feet above the sea. The bees, however had other ideas. They continued to attack Pierre and Frankie whenever their heads appeared above the surface. Diving and keeping underwater for long periods until the bees called off their attack was no mean feat. At one point I thought that Pierre had drowned, considering the length of time he stayed submerged in the water, just to avoid the bees.

Eventually the bees gave up, leaving a spluttering Pierre and Frankie to rue their intrusion. Watching all this going on from the beach, we just could not do anything to help. Both had swollen faces, fat lips and closed eyes within minutes. The bees even got to several places that are better left undisclosed.

Originally named the Coronation Cup, the East African Safari was a motor rally held every year in the rainy months. It ranged over the three countries of Kenya, Uganda and Tanzania, and became for us boys, the highlight of the Easter period. It was very well supported by overseas competitors, rally car manufacturers and private entries from all over the world. This was an exciting time for us in the annual calendar of events.

Pop usually arranged to take us to a spot just outside Cosy Café in Dar es Salaam city centre from which to view the sometimes frenzied activity at close quarters as the cars were refuelled, tyres changed and generally kept in running order.

From the courtyard of the café while eating and drinking we had a magnificent view of all the rally cars. Pierre's love of cars must have been fired by the vast array of high-powered rally cars all around us.

The East African Safari Rally is considered one of the most, if not the most, gruelling auto race in the world. It was, and still is to some extent, the testing ground for reliability in production cars. Up to 90 percent of the cars entered in the race never finished. The course itself has varied from year to year, averaging from 3100 to 4000 miles in length, originally travelling through Kenya, Tanzania, and Uganda.

So what makes this race so tough?

African roads are not for the squeamish. First there are the hazards of wildlife and farm animals on the course. Then there's the earth of Africa itself, which comes in every size and type, from a fine dust that clogs cars and blinds drivers in its huge clouds to bowling-ball sized boulders that punish both drivers and suspension components in equal measure. Then come the stone-throwing youths all along the route, trying their best to hit the cars whizzing by their doorsteps and villages.

True, you can find some of these conditions on other rally courses, but the Safari Rally has one thing that the other rallies really don't, and that's very heavy, almost monsoon type of rain. The race is held over the Easter long weekend, which falls somewhere between the end of March and the middle of April. This also generally coincides with the beginning of the rainy season. Rain and red African earth combine to form mud. This is no mud puddle, this is a slicker-than-ice gumbo that sinks cars like quicksand in bad weather, and dries hard like stucco in the sun.

Rain is the wildcard in the Safari, and you can't really prepare for it. Some years the course is dry, allowing lots of teams to finish. Other years, the course has been so badly flooded that stages have to be re-routed or cancelled outright, and teams have slogged for hours over a section that should have taken minutes.

Early competing makes included the Volkswagen Beetle, Mercedes, Ford Zephyr, Opel, Austin, Peugeot, Fiat and Datsuns. Drivers originally started out at three different locations and finished in Nairobi. The rally was renamed the East African Safari Rally in 1960, and kept that name until 1973 when it became the Safari Rally.

We were taken by Pop to view the array of high-powered rally cars as they stopped for refuelling just outside Cosy Café in the city centre. It was exciting to view the mud-splattered cars at close quarters. The local drivers, the Joginder Singh brothers, dominated the rally for years. Overseas guests included Pat and Eric Carlsson driving their Volvo. The old-fashioned Volkswagen Beetle with its rear engine starred in many races.

These cars had to endure rough country roads with wild, free-roaming game to contend with, just as we had to when travelling to Arusha to see our grandmother. Despite its age the Beetle had to endure these rough country roads and seemed to have the capabilities of virtually floating, or so it seemed, on the many flooded roads. Occasionally competitors might also have to run the gauntlet of local spectators showing their displeasure by throwing stones, but this was very infrequent.

It was all very exciting as a youngster to be there and be part of the action and see our local drivers. Our love for cars today came from Pop.

Whenever I return to Dar es Salaam my visit conjures up a tingle of this excitement as we visit all the restaurants and familiar places, and of course Cosy Café.

CHAPTER SIX

Rocking into the sixties

The Cosy Café was on the ground floor and courtyard of a small but swish and imposing building in Dar es Salaam which had been built when the area was a German colony. In our time it had always been the Cosy Café and was one of our favourite places for drinks and ice creams. It happened to be located centrally on a very well-known corner in the centre of Dar, with a commanding view of everybody going about their business. This is the place everybody wanted to be seen in. Here in the city centre Pop and Mum and their relatives and friends would meet, often sitting outside in the evenings for drinks and joyous conversation and laughter.

It also offered the most delicious ice creams of all flavours, and the world's tastiest samosa, "sambusa", as we locals called it.

One thing that binds Indians and others around the world is a crisp, spicy, fried, stuffed patty – the samosa. This triangular delight, though relished traditionally with afternoon tea, is an all-time hit, now used as an appetiser in restaurants throughout the world.

The basic samosa generally consist of wheat flour and mashed potatoes mixed with green coriander or mint chutney, but it is also enjoyed with ketchup, and even curried masala, pickles and sliced onions. However, as they have moved around the world they can be found with infinitely varied fillings to suite local tastes. You can get fillings of selected fruits, cottage cheese and dried fruits and nuts such as cashew, pistachio, almonds, raisins and different varieties of non-vegetarian stuffing like minced mutton, beef or chicken.

A freshly-fried, crisp brown samosa, exuding stimulating aroma, is such a tempting, palatable experience that you cannot resist. Dry mini samosas filled with softened and ground lentils, dried fruit and spices, have shelf lives of several weeks.

In the evenings, we would sit outside chatting and savouring the scent of the jasmine trees in the shade of swaying palms and exotic tropical plants. I am sure that it was the bougainvillea plants with their breathtakingly colourful bracts of red, yellow, pink and white intertwining with the jasmine plants that provoked both my and Pierre's enduring love of horticulture and of exotic plants.

Cosy Café was a hub for social activity and parties. Seating would be outside in the evening cool breeze under the sweet, fragrant white jasmine plant climbing over the walls and structures to provide a gorgeous canopy. Palm trees, leaves and exotic tropical plants swayed in the evening breeze. The fragrance of the jasmine's star-shaped flowers is the most intoxicating perfume imaginable.

Unhappily, while the building remains to this day, the Cosy Café is no more than a lasting, happy and rewarding memory.

However enjoyable our drinks and ice creams were at the Cosy Café, for Pierre, our brother Andy and me, its other very significant effect on the Naya family was sparked by its having the only juke box in town. It spurred inspiration that became, simply, life changing, and the café achieved iconic status in our eyes. What an inspirational joy. Pierre was completely bowled over by this magnificent sound of the electric guitar playing rock n' roll on this juke box.

There were no televisions in those days and the only music available was the radio and the usual BBC World Service and local stations. In these circumstances, to hear Cliff Richard and the Shadows for the first time on early recordings was just something else. Belting out tunes such as *Move It, Dynamite, Apache, Living Doll, Please Don't Tease, Gee Whiz It's You* and many others just took them to a different world. There were also the early recordings of Elvis Presley and *Jailhouse Rock* and Bill Haley's *Rock Around the Clock* and other singers like Chuck Berry. Our musical world simply erupted. It was to kick-start both Pierre's and Andy's musical careers.

Listening to the raw guitar sound of the Fender Stratocaster of Hank Marvin, the lead guitarist of the Shadows, excited Pierre and Andy into wanting to create that magical sound and gallop behind the trend. They would sit for hours listening to the juke box playing these great hits, both imagining that they too were playing the guitars. In time how right I was, as in no time at all, Pierre found the love of his life, the electric guitar.

Neither my parents nor I made any pretence to be musicians, but we would certainly go anywhere for a good dance and to enjoy the good company of others. Disco had not been discovered in our region of the world in the early sixties. At weddings and formal dances, professional older musicians would play, often as a quartet on piano, saxophone, bass and drums. Proper musicians they were.

Listening to this new rock guitar sound had a tremendous impact on Pierre and Andy, who, with their natural ability and musical ears, could appreciate the direction in which it would take them. This was while they were still at school, and it amazes me to this day. It was all started by that single magical juke box and the special atmosphere it generated in the Cosy Café. Its memory still haunts me. Pierre grew into an accomplished and versatile guitarist. This stood him well in later years, as everywhere he went, the guitar was not far from him.

It will not go away and when I visit the city I try to stand outside the café to reminisce, with anyone who will tolerate my enthusiasm, about the good old days listening to the Shadows, who became our first heroes. Such are my memories that if you were to ask me for my favourite place, without hesitation, it would be the Cosy Café in the city of Dar es Salaam, Tanzania.

While this music revolution was taking place here in Dar, something of the same nature was taking place thousands of miles away in London. The 2i's coffee house, situated at 59 Old Compton Street, near Piccadilly Circus in London's Soho District, which was first run by two Iranian brothers, hence the name of the café, was all the craze. There was a rock n' roll revolution taking place there simultaneously, just as in our Cosy Café coffee bar in Dar es Salaam.

The 2i's was one of those coffee bars that sprang up all over Soho. It was decorated plainly with linoleum floors and formica tables, so becoming a model for many classic Formica cafés to come during that decade. The tiny room could hold no more than twenty people, but in September 1956, rock singer Tony Hicks was spotted by an impresario who was looking for someone or something that would set London's West End alight. During a 2i's session with the Vipers, Decca, the record company signed him up, and Hicks became the first British rock n' roll star, better known as Tommy Steele.

The story of his discovery turned the 2i's coffee bar into a goldmine, and its reputation began to spread. It became the focal point for rock n' roll enthusiasts. Soon patrons would stay for the entire evening, ordering no more than one cup of coffee, so an admission charge of one shilling was levied.

The 2i's Coffee Bar became a showcase, a cattle market for young hopefuls. All of them would be assessed by impresarios, agents and record company men. A very young and upcoming Cliff Richard paid a visit to the club looking for a touring band. The new members of the Shadows, Hank and Bruce, all met and played there, and later found fame. A Green Plaque was at last unveiled to commemorate this legendary venue which witnessed the birth and rise of the British rock scene. When, later on, we arrived in London, we made our own pilgrimage to this iconic coffee bar to relive our memories.

Back in Dar, Piérre and Andy were teaching themselves to play the guitar. Andy picked up his skills from his brother. Pierre's flare quickly moved him to find a talented Mauritian family group who were quite talented musicians, playing the rhythm guitar. Music was in Pierre's blood by now.

They practised and improved quickly, modelling themselves on the Shadows, and becoming well known in Dar as the Blue Shadows. Three of the group, together with Pierre, were still schoolboys. They dressed in long-sleeved blue satin shirts, which shimmered when the stage spotlight focused on them, and regulation black trousers. Pierre played an electric Hofner red and white guitar, Tony Gonsalves played the drums and George DeSouza was the bass guitarist and lead singer. The lead guitarist was Jocelyn Allet, also with a Hofner. He was the eldest son of this family, with a day-time job as an electrician. George today lives in Canada and has shared the stage with such names as Tom Jones and Tony Bennett, to name but two.

Lloyd Montalban was another member, who added maturity to the group on mouth organ, bongos and percussion. Amplification was by the famous Vox amplifiers.

The famous red and white Fender Stratocaster immortalised by Hank Marvin was not available at that time in all of East Africa. Hardly surprising, as Hank himself had just only got one ordered for him from America by Cliff Richard and played on all of their earlier hits. This guitar of Hank's would cost a fortune now – it is in the possession of Bruce Welch, rhythm guitarist of the Shadows. I'd love to get my hands on it!

Naturally they modelled themselves on the Shadows and Pierre modelled his guitar-playing style on Hank's. As Cliff's backing band and a popular instrumental group in their own right, the Shadows' influence on young would-be musicians, such as Pierre and Andy in Dar es Salaam, was inspirational.

The Blue Shadows practised every minute they had at Jocelyn's first-floor house in Dar. This was a very fulfilling but manic period of activity, enjoyed especially by passers-by, who stopped in the main street to listen to this new sound in the music scene of Dar which took off very quickly. They played all Cliff's and the Shadows' numbers as well as those of other artists such as Buddy Holly, Elvis, the Beatles and Bill Haley and the Comets. As the band's popularity spread they soon added many dance numbers to their repertoire, presented in an eclectic mix of styles and sounds. Their repertoire held no boundaries. They provided the music at weddings, birthday parties and other functions right across the city, held in local bars hosting a knees-up and venues in large hotels and private clubs. In a very short time, their versatility and broad spectrum of music brought them fame in Dar es Salaam. They packed cinemas and halls, giving rock concerts, played on national radio and made their own recordings.

Very soon the Blue Shadows, had many loyal and faithful followers all over the city. My feelings were of admiration and pride in Pierre's achievements, but I envied the ease with which he attracted his admirers. How he made time for his schooling and homework amazes me. I feel sure he had a few teachers with reason to take him to task.

The irony was that many of these same teachers would enjoy the band playing themselves while they sat and listened or drank and danced the night away.

This was a great time in our lives and Pop and Mother were extremely proud of Pierre's achievements. Yes, the band members were paid for their endeavours, but it all went to improve their musical instruments and equipment. It was not done for money, but pure enjoyment and showmanship.

As happens sometimes, the younger brothers of Pierre and Jocelyn began to get itchy feet and decided that they wanted to play like their seniors. I knew that I was not cut out to be a musician, but three brothers of Jocelyn and one of mine formed what became "The Fentoms", playing in the same style as the Blue Shadows.

My younger brother Andy was the rhythm guitarist and singer and of Jocelyn's brothers, Findlay became the drummer, and in later years was the leading drummer in East Africa, holding concerts playing solo. Carl turned his hand to the bass guitar and Ben became the lead guitarist. They were joined by Maurice Goosen, who was the other guitarist and singer. Carl today still entertains in the five-star luxury hotels in Mauritius, performing with his show band.

Practising in our household was a bit of a problem, so as one group finished the other group took over both the household and instruments. The junior band borrowed the senior band's instrument when available until, much further down the line, they had their own.

Friendly rivalry and the promise of stardom ensured that eventually, the Fentoms got just as many gigs as the senior group and, eventually, camp followers.

So, the music scene in Dar was dominated by these talented musicians. The junior band followed its elder group by playing live to cinema audiences and making radio recordings and live shows. Chox, Odeon and Avalon were all large cinemas with several hundred seating capacity. The atmosphere was just fantastic, with the band playing on the dedicated stage. All these building still exist today, except the Odeon, although none are cinemas today.

All this, I must emphasise, was happening in Dar while Pierre and Andy, were still at school. It shows the talent that Pierre possessed even at that very early age.

These radio broadcasts would reach even more people in Dar and surrounding towns. On Dar es Salaam radio station, both bands would make weekly live appearances. Furthermore, the German radio presenter and producer introduced a live programme where the boys would be asked to assess and give comments on the latest records released, in a format similar to that adopted by David Jacob's *Juke Box Jury* shown on the UK television network.

Tanganyika Broadcasting Corporation was based in the Pugu Road area of Dar, quite near to where Pop had his lorry workshop as you drove towards the international airport. This radio station came into existence in July 1956, transmitting on medium wave with a signal strength which was the most powerful in East Africa at that time. It provided almost territory wide coverage, and reception reports were received from countries as distant as Japan, Finland and New Zealand. The TBC station relied on international reports such as those from the BBC for programmes both in English and Swahili.

Approximately one hundred people were employed by the radio station, with well-trained Africans who were at ease with its operation. It was estimated that 500,000 people were listening to the station regularly. With independence, the TBC was renamed Radio Tanzania Dar es Salaam.

So music making and guitars had risen in a relatively short time from an interesting pastime prompted by that juke box in the Cosy Café to the overriding business in the Naya household. To this day Andy, who lives in Spain still, earns his living playing at gigs and singing, and perfecting the beautiful sound of the Fender Stratocaster in the style of Hank Marvin. The Stratocaster is just one of the many electric and acoustic guitars he has collected over the intervening years, with a variety of speakers, amplifiers and other gizmos.

Politics and mutiny

After gaining independence in 1961, the first objective of the then ruling President, Dr Julius Nyerere, and his party was to introduce nationalisation in pursuit of its socialist objectives. It led to a period of quite dramatic change in Tanzania as this political agenda was vigorously adopted.

What happened in Tanzania was part of the more general trend followed by some African politicians being freed from colonial rule as political leaders achieved positions of authority in their countries. It took time for changes to be introduced in each country and for them to be felt in the wider population. An extreme example of the political trend was Uganda, where dramatic changes were introduced by President Idi Amin, long after our family had left Tanzania. He came to power in 1971 and gained notoriety worldwide for discreditable reasons in his pursuit of his political and personal aims.

One common but very unsettling measure introduced in Tanzania, which directly affected employment prospects, was the political move to introduce Africans into jobs previously held by non-Africans and whites. Across the country this very quickly introduced uncertainty about the future for those affected by this pro-African employment bias. The major consequence to employers from the Asian and European community was their loss of well integrated staff and its replacement by Africans with less company and business experience. The positions of the employers themselves became equally difficult or unsustainable and many were forced to start winding down their businesses. These were the people who previously had been the hub and catalyst of the country's growth.

These were very unsettling times. We became depressed as life, as we knew it, started its downward spiral for the worse and took on a frightening aspect, especially for those of us born and settled in Tanzania, our adopted country.

In 1971 a military coup in Uganda brought Idi Amin to power. Eight months later it was announced that all Asians, including 12,000 still awaiting citizenship, were to leave the country within 90 days. It was later stated that only non-citizen Asians were obliged to leave, but subsequently some 15,000 Ugandan passport holders had their passports withdrawn and others were intimidated by Amin's soldiers.

Within the last six weeks of the period of the ultimatum, 50,000 Asians left Uganda, with no property and £55 in cash each. 27,000 of them fled to Britain, which temporarily waived its immigration laws to deal with the crisis. 10,000 went to India (including 6,000 UK citizens), 6,000 to Canada, 4,000 to United Nation camps throughout Europe, and others to the USA, Pakistan and elsewhere, including Kenya and Malawi.

While the commercial climate was altering in Tanzania, one event stood out as a critical turning point in the consideration of our future prospects as a family. This was the Military Mutiny in 1964 in Tanzania. It showed that the confidence of the then ruling party Tanzania African National Union, in the neutrality of the armed forces was unfounded.

It started on January 19th 1964 when the first battalion left its Colito barracks, arrested British officers and took key installations in Dar es Salaam, including the radio station, police headquarters, the airport and State House. The Tabora-based second battalion joined the mutiny two days later. The mutiny was accompanied by widespread looting, which particularly affected the Asian population, as its community in Dar es Salaam became a prime target. New British appointments had given some in the army the impression that Tanganyikan NCOs might never be promoted. This mismanagement seemed to have tipped a balance, driving a group of about ten long-serving NCOs and other ranks to plan a mutiny.

The plotters were led by a sergeant. Soon after the mutineers had taken control of Colito Barracks, they called for a general meeting. They had decided that the new-style army would be run not by themselves, but by the officers selected by the general acclaim of the soldiers. Those chosen would be promoted to a suitable rank and would run the army under the general guidance of the mutineers.

Were any of the mutineers to be selected, they would serve in their new role without admitting their part in the mutiny. The most contentious issue was the selection of the new Brigadier, in overall command of the army. Who would wear the coveted red-banded hat taken from Flagstaff House? An obvious choice would have been Captain Nyirenda, by now locked up in the guardroom cell, along with other officers. He was one of the most senior and best qualified Tanganyikan officers, and could have easily slipped into the role. However, it counted against him that he was a Nyasa, rather than from one of the main tribes. It was eventually agreed that he should be released from his cell, but should only retain his present company command, without promotion.

In negotiations with the government, the mutineers demanded both the expulsion of the British serving officers and higher pay. The

British government was called to help, as the president went into hiding, rumoured to be on board HMS *Centaur*, a British ship moored a few miles offshore, with its Royal Marine Commando units on board.

The marines landed by helicopters and attacked Colito barracks, surprising the African army. Three African soldiers were killed and the rest just gave up, effectively suppressing the mutineers. The President's position had not been in jeopardy, as he appeared to think, but this mutiny was all about pay demands.

During the early afternoon of 21st January came the dramatic news that President Nyerere had reappeared and was broadcasting to the nation in Swahili. He told the nation that a slight crisis had occurred in Dar es Salaam and had ended the same day. He did not give the nation the reasons why this crisis occurred. He tried to dispel the anxiety of the people, saying it was all false that there was no Government and that he was still around and had not disappeared, contrary to suggestions. He said that it was a very minor affair and people should not worry too much. He went on to ask the people to stop spreading alarmist rumours. He pointed out that there were others who used this as an excuse to break into people houses and plunder people's property. He tried to reassure the nation that there was still a government. He sent his condolences to the families of the three soldiers killed and said it was a day of disgrace and hoped that there would not be a repetition of this disgraceful behaviour. He thanked all the people who helped to stop this disgrace from spreading beyond limits and hope that our country will not witness any repetition of such a disgrace either tomorrow or the next day. This broadcast did not reassure everyone, least of all my parents.

Speaking on the day the British landed, Nyerere sought to explain why the Tanganyikan Government had to call for help from the British Government. He wanted to speak to all the people of Tanzania. He went on to say that there had been trouble in Dar es Salaam which arose out of some grievances of the 1st Battalion of the Tanganyikan Rifles. He promised the army that the Government would consider their justified claims and the troops appeared to be satisfied. On the same day they went back to their barracks, but they had already committed a most serious offence - mutiny.

After this grave offence had been committed by our troops, a number of civilians committed offences such as looting, and in the work of restoring order after this some lives were lost. Nyerere wanted the troops to repent, but some of them would not admit that they had done anything wrong, and when he asked the leaders to ask their soldiers not to wear battledress but to go back to ceremonial uniform, some of the leaders refused.

He went on to say that an army which does not obey the laws and orders of the people's government is not an army of that country and it is a danger to its own nation. He finally decided that there was only one thing which could be done, and that was to disarm all the troops and punish the ringleaders most severely. The only force we could deploy in this task of disarming the army was the field force of the police. But this force was already depleted because we had previously sent some of them to Zanzibar to help maintain law and order there. The president gave this as a reason to ask for help.

He decided to ask Britain for help. Fortunately Britain agreed. This morning therefore, he said, the 1st Battalion of the Tanganyika Rifles here in Dar es Salaam were disarmed in their barracks. Those troops in the city handed over their arms to the police force. It is possible that there are some soldiers who have not yet handed in their arms. If so they must go at once to the nearest police station and give up their weapons.

All is now calm and no one should be frightened by the British troops in the city or the planes and helicopters flying around.

Clearly it is essential that we should build up the Republic's army once again. I call upon all members of the TANU Youth League wherever they are to go to the local TANU office and enrol themselves. From this group we shall try to build a nucleus of the new army of the Republic of Tanganyika.

He went on to say that already there is foolish talk that the British have come back to rule Tanganyika again. This is rubbish. I asked the British Government to help us in the same way as I would have asked our neighbours to help us if this had been possible. Asking for help in this way is not something to be proud of. I do not want any person to think that I was happy in making this request. This whole week has been a week of most grievous shame for our nation. But those who brought this shame upon us are those who tried to intimidate our nation at the point of a gun.

The torch of freedom will still burn on the top of Mount Kilimanjaro. President Nyerere disbanded the army in months.

This did not fool my mother's intention and emotions, and on reflection I feel today that this whole episode in particular was the last straw on the camel's back as far as she was concerned. Why should we jeopardise our safety any longer? Our life style had already deteriorated significantly, creating pressure on our parents too great for them to endure for much longer.

While writing this particular chapter about the mutiny in Dar, I spoke to two people living here in Hereford, who were present, residing and working in Dar es Salaam when this scenario occurred. This is their recollections of their experiences.

Derrick and Ann Pitt, a British husband and wife, and their young daughter, aged three, were living in the European area of Oyster Bay in Dar. Derrick was an accountant who worked for the British Civil Overseas Service, and he was posted to Tanzania from 1956-67 to work in the Government's Treasury and Revenue Office in Dar. This, according to Derrick, was a prime and treasured posting, if not just for the prized pensionable appointment and promotion prospects. He was 29. Ann worked as a governmental secretary while bringing up a young family.

On the day of the mutiny, their next-door neighbour, who was the British personal pilot of President Nyerere, knocked on their bedroom window at 6 am and urgently asked them not to go to work that day as there was a mutiny going on. He was asked to take the president out, so he obviously had inside information which the public did not have. The small European community living in Oyster Bay were recommended to stay indoors until further news was known. Ann says that she was extremely frightened for the family and daughter Helen, and was listening constantly to the radio and the BBC overseas service news, which highlighted the mutiny to be much worse than it was. Derrick, at this, said to Ann "where is your British bulldog spirit?" and was not alarmed in the least. If you knew Derrick, he was not a racist in any form in his remark.

"What are we going to do?" asked Ann of Derrick. To which he replied "nothing". He had a shower, shave and some breakfast and wandered about the houses on foot, speaking to neighbours and seeking information. As they lived only about three miles from the army barracks, they did hear gunshots.

Their ayah, or staff, named Nibwene, reassured Ann that Helen, their young daughter, would be safe whatever the consequences, because she reassured them, that she would take the daughter with her and hide in the countryside, so no harm would befall her.

The neighbours mounted a security watch all night, taking two-hour shifts, sitting on their verandas on the lookout. Derrick drew the short straw and his shift was from 2 am to 4 am. All their cars were ready for any dash they had to make. Emergency bags of essentials were packed and were at the ready at a moment's notice. Derrick tells of his best friend and neighbour Len, packing only all

63

his Playboy magazines! This remained a talking point and source of laughter for days to come.

Another European neighbour of theirs, a captain in the King's African Army, went into hiding, never to be seen again, and left a deserted house, which neighbours had to pack and secure. All the house staff appeared daily as usual for work.

I include this little story as told to me as I find it fascinating to hear another family's opinion on this mutiny which involved us all.

There is a touch of irony in that this same president who wanted rapid changes following his achieving independence to pursue his socialist agenda should seek protection and help from the British on Her Majesty's ship when alarmed by this mutiny. Also this very president, who pressurised our way of life so much that we felt the need to leave our native country, should follow us to the UK to seek medical help in our National Health Service when he was ill, with a blood disorder. He subsequently died in a London hospital in 1999. The double standards madden me.

To Pierre and me, the skirmish between the British and Tanzanian troops was the touchstone for the military experience that started quite soon afterwards and lasted for much of our working lives. Our family had long held British citizenship and therefore had held British passports for generations, since the days of British colonial rule.

Mother decided it was no longer safe for us to continue living in Tanzania and made the decision that we would move to the UK to make a new life for ourselves. Other friends and relatives were also preparing to move and some had already done so, some returning to the Seychelles, others to Australia and a few as far afield as Canada. At no stage in these times did Pierre indicate that he wanted to join the British Army and serve as a medic. I think events such as the exploits of the Royal Marines in suppressing the military mutiny must have had an impact on Pierre.

Robert, being the eldest brother, was the first to up sticks and fly to the UK. He immediately joined the Royal Green Jackets, one of Her Majesty's fiercest fighting regiments, subsequently serving in Borneo and other far-flung places in the world, for six years. Pierre and a close friend of the family called Danny Wilson flew next to London and stayed with friends, a few months before the rest of the family.

Pierre enlisted soon after into the Royal Army Medical Corps on the 21st June 1964 to start his illustrious military career, at the age of 19 years. Again, he never indicated that that was what he wanted to do, so it was a surprise to us all.

Mum, younger brother Andrew and sister Marianne and I were soon to follow, leaving Tanzania in December 1964 by ship, the Lloyd Triestino passenger liner M/V *Africa*.

Father and Frankie were left behind to follow us just a few months later, after settling things in Dar es Salaam.

Reflecting on this period of our lives, everything, including our education, just came to a halt. One possible option was to emigrate to Australia through the arrangement that encouraged migrants, at a passage cost of £10, to go to live and work in Australia. Mother had all the paperwork sorted, until Pop decided otherwise by delaying the completion of the necessary forms. Who knows - we might all have been Aussies!

Mother had to simply leave her property to the Africans. She was not allowed to sell it, nor did she receive compensation from the government. Imagine how bitter she must have felt with her dreams shattered.

I know what a furore compensation claims would now cause if it was the other way round and we as British had to pay compensation as the Mau Mau veterans are now trying to achieve from the claimed, atrocities that took place in Kenya a long time ago, under Jomo Kenyatta.

Yes, I do feel bitter and somehow sad about the way things beyond our control took over our lives. However, being forced into our move to the UK gave us avenues and opportunity to further our careers and provided the foundation for the lives we now lead outside Tanzania.

So we had departed Dar es Salaam and Tanzania in December 1964. We left our adopted home, our past, friends and remaining relatives, carrying suitcases of our belongings with all our memories. It is impossible to think that we might have done so without shedding a tear as we left, so full of apprehension about what might lie ahead of us in our lives in the UK.

All our remaining relatives and friends, who were soon to follow, had seen us off at the ferry and passenger terminal, just outside our wonderful cathedral that had been such a significant part of our lives thus far. They waved us farewell, with tears streaming down their faces. It was a heart-breaking departure for us all, leaving what was for us and, for me, still is 'home'. What a daunting feeling we all had.

I wrote this lyric while thinking back to that emotional time in our lives. It expresses the ever-changing flashes of thoughts of the departing boy for the safety of home, the imaginings of the future, the hopes and probable failures for a new life, how will he fit in, where will he fit in, what can he be proud of, how does he communicate, how does he make a living, where shall he live? It might even make a song…

Cool guy, don't lie to yourself. Don't run off to Europe, you can also be successful here, even by growing tomatoes.

It's best to know what you are doing. Cool men haven't gone to school.

They don't even know you know English. Just two words, yes and no. Is that all you are able to say on the street?

What will you be speaking there then, cool guy?

Think first before going, cool guy, so that you won't rue that day. Will you not be a mute person where you are going?

The truth is that you don't want to work, that you want to go with the times, but what times are these, cool guy?

You don't even have a tartan to wrap yourself in, your shirt is worth ten thousand shillings, your trousers are worth ten thousand shillings, and your shoes are worth twenty thousand shillings. Cool guy, think again.

Will you cover yourself with your clothes on a cold night? Take any kind of job, here, so that you can earn some money.

Take care my cool friend, and good luck.

CHAPTER EIGHT

A new life in the UK

So we boarded the M/V *Africa*, bound for Trieste in Italy, and onwards then by train to London. This ship ran a regular return scheduled voyage from Trieste to Cape Town, South Africa and back again, calling at major ports along the eastern coast of Africa, including Dar es Salaam, Mombasa, Mogadishu, Aden and Port Said. At the end of our voyage north, we would stop in Venice before docking at the home port of Trieste, where we anticipated disembarking.

The liner, moored and looking serenely inviting, waited for us in the beautiful natural harbour of Dar es Salaam. We were off on a real adventure. To begin it we had to board the embarkation boat from our much-loved playground jetty where, close by, we had spent so many enjoyable hours of our youth fishing from the shore and swimming in the beautiful warm, clear waters.

Leaving those of our family who had come to wave us away with many more friends ashore was heart wrenching. Passing through the harbour entrance was nearly as bad, with crowds of people waving away their family or friends, some of whom they might never see again. But our personal turmoil subsided as we made our way to the open sea, replaced by our anticipation of what lay ahead of us.

This Italian-owned and crewed liner had about two hundred and fifteen crew, not quite as many as there were passengers in the tourist class section, in which we travelled, which could accommodate two hundred and ninety eight passengers. The Naya family settled into one large comfortable cabin and found, in talking to other passengers, who were mainly European, that some were also setting out on a life-changing voyage to pastures new.

In some respects our time on board felt like a holiday. The voyage was much more than that; a life-changing expedition with the outcome in doubt unless we really found our feet quickly when we arrived in London. However, for the time being, our holiday was to enjoy our new luxurious surroundings, sailing to new places and being served with wonderful Italian food, which we hadn't eaten before.

The aperitif and table wine at dinner on white, washed and starched table linen did make it feel as though we were in the lap of luxury. The food was just marvellous, and as the crew members knew we were relocating our homes, they looked after us very well. One member lent us his own personal radio to listen to for the whole voyage. Although mother was very grateful for this generous gesture she considered it a little too overgenerous to let us retain it for the whole of the voyage. But our long faces might have given the game away.

As the ship made its way along the African coast, stopping off at places like Mombasa and Mogadishu, it sailed unmolested through waters off Somalia which today are infested with hostile pirates.

Stopping off at Aden was a very exciting experience. There was a tremendous buzz of activity created by frenzied bartering of Arab touts trying to sell souvenirs from their tiny boats as they clung to this huge luxury liner. Baskets of goods were being sent up the liner's side with ropes attached. I wondered what would happen if they had one dishonest buyer not sending the cash back down.

I had only heard of the Suez Canal in books and history lessons.

Going through it for the first time in my life was awe-inspiring. Seeing the wonderful Pyramids in the distance made it majestic.

At some points the ship appeared to be touching the sides of the canal while navigating the traffic and obstacles. My memory of the green lushness of the occasional oasis with its palm and date trees stays vividly with me to this day. However, my recollections of the canal transit compare very favourably with those of the rough seas we encountered while in the Mediterranean and its effects on me.

It was not a pleasant crossing. We had left Dar when it was approaching the hottest time of the year with temperatures soaring to 30-40° C, so what a shock it was for us to experience our first taste of northern hemisphere winter temperatures, especially as we did not have any appropriate cold-weather clothes. We just seemed to be approaching cooler, colder weather as our journey progressed. Oh to be back in the warmth of Dar.

We were due to disembark in Trieste at the end of the voyage, but when we were in Venice, the ship's penultimate destination, we were informed of an imminent strike on the French railway network which was expected to be a prolonged dispute. Mother made the decision to end our journey then and there, and we disembarked in Venice.

We then had the problem of getting us and our luggage across the city to the main railway station. Apparently, the only means of doing so was to use a gondola, packed to the gunwales with suitcases. While this may have been the only option it turned out to be an expensive one, and to this day, I feel that my mother lost out to a wilier operator.

Our journey continued by rail to Calais, then by ferry to Dover, then on to London Victoria station. From there we took a taxi to a friend's house in Tooting Broadway in South London.

We had arrived, shivering in the cold, in London on the 4th December 1964. The whole trip took four weeks. Yes, we were all extremely apprehensive, anxious even, but also fairly confident that the future would be better than the past we had left behind in Dar es Salaam.

Pierre had already spent a few months in the army by this time, and appearing to enjoy his new adventure. We thought we knew from his letters what to expect. In reality, the consequences of tearing up our roots and leaving home, childhood and birthplace, friends and relations behind to form a new life abroad were totally unimaginable.

CHAPTER NINE

Pierre joins the
Royal Army Medical Corps

On the 21st June 1964, Pierre enlisted in the Royal Army Medical Corps (RAMC) on a twenty-two year engagement service as 23952578 Pte. P. H. R. Naya. He was aged 19 years.

In 1857 the Medical Staff Corps was reorganised into the Army Hospital Corps, although it reverted back to its former name in 1884 and by 1889 there were two distinct organisations within the Army Medical Services, the Medical Staff Corps and the Medical Staff (i.e. the officers). These two separate organisations were reorganised into one Corps, the Royal Army Medical Corps, by Royal Warrant on the 23rd June 1898.

With the formation of the RAMC, medical officers were granted the same rank structure as the rest of the British Army and assumed full executive and administration responsibility. Three months later RAMC personnel were serving in the Sudan, and only one year after its formation the RAMC was fully committed in the Anglo-Boer War.

Since the Victoria Cross was instituted in 1856, there have been

29 Victoria Crosses and two bars awarded to medical personnel. A bar, indicating a subsequent award, has been awarded only on three occasions.

Our Corp motto "In Arduis Fidelis" (Faithful in Adversity), is an inspiration to all members who have served in the Corp.

Initial army basic training for a period of sixteen weeks took place at Keogh Barracks, Ash Vale, a training depot just outside Aldershot in Hampshire. Basic training, as many readers will testify, included physical training, drill instruction, military law, hygiene and basic first aid, weapons training, military skills, aspects of chemical warfare, initiative testing, education examinations, medical tests and much more.

After this initial sixteen weeks training at the depot you would have an interview with the Technical Training Officer to choose your particular technical trade. Pierre chose and was accepted to be an Operating Theatre Technician (OTT) and could be deployed to any one of several military hospitals both in the UK and abroad.

There were many other trades available for young recruits to choose from in the medical corps, including nursing, laboratory technician, physiotherapy, administration clerk, combat medical technician and hygienist, just to name a few.

Pierre's very first posting to continue his training in his chosen trade was to the military hospital in Colchester, Essex, where he would remain for the next six years.

While there, Pierre met and married Nina, a lovely lady also in the army, who was studying to be a nurse in the Queen Alexandra's Royal Army Nursing Corps. They were married on the 10th December 1965 and remained very happily married for 47 years, a record any married couple would be proud to achieve.

They produced four beautiful daughters in Juliette, twins Ginette and Alison and Nicola. Alison has Pierre's artistic talents and produces great work of art in exhibitions in the UK. All his daughters have provided him with much loved and cherished grandchildren.

Both Pierre and Nina had a very affectionate nick name for one another, 'Pomme', which stayed with them throughout their married lives.

At the completion of training, the custom then was to serve for two or three years in one posting, then move on to another military hospital. The British Army Medical Services ran its own hospitals both in the UK and abroad, spread widely to provide specialist support wherever it might be needed. At that time there were hospitals abroad in Hong Kong, Cyprus, Singapore, Nepal and several spread in West Germany, namely Berlin, Hanover, Munster, Rinteln and Iserlohn. Today, all these have been shut down for economic reasons highlighted by the Ministry of Defence as part of its 'Options of Change' programme introduced a few years ago. What a daft idea, as events in later years have proved. In my view the politicians and others had it totally wrong.

Pierre's later postings included two separate periods in Hong Kong, Berlin and the Queen Elizabeth Military Hospital in Woolwich, London. Two further postings found him at the Cambridge Military Hospital in Aldershot, our Operating Theatre Training School, where he would be involved in training new recruits in operating theatre techniques. Pierre was a good teacher and many of his students have given him praise for this. His philosophy was not to shout and bawl his head off, but to be calm and clinical, thereby gaining many admirers.

Pierre continued to serve in the Royal Army Medical Corps for twenty two years, during which time of service he was awarded the Military Medal, one of the highest awards for gallantry and bravery in the British Army, for his deeds in the Falklands War in 1982. He retired from the army in the rank of Staff Sergeant with distinguished conduct.

Here I hope to give readers a glimpse of the wide training and scope of employment gained in his, and later my career, and training in the Royal Army Medical Corps (RAMC) as an Operating Theatre Technician (OTT).

Under the general heading of "Preparation of the anaesthetic and operating rooms of an operating theatre", the OTT has a detailed and extensive knowledge of all anaesthetic drugs, their use and possible complications, machinery such as ventilators, monitoring and all apparatus as well as all surgical instrumentation, their names and how they are used and for what type of surgery in a wide range of surgical procedures. He has a wide and detailed knowledge of the ranges of hazards and complications arising during and after surgery and how to rectify this. He is able to assist a surgeon and anaesthetist at all highly specialised procedures and care of patients. He can take charge of an operating theatre, supervising the work and training of junior OTTs, nursing sisters and junior medical staff, trainee surgeons and anaesthetists.

As an operating theatre technician he is responsible for and manages the Central Sterile Supply Department (CSSD) and the resupply, care, of cleaning and resterilising instruments, with a wide technical and detailed knowledge of sterilizers.

He can organise stores' requirements and maintain detailed records. He has an advanced knowledge of fractures and their treatment, and works unsupervised in running a plaster clinic applying the whole range of plaster of Paris and frames to a variety of fractures.

The army OTT is highly trained in human anatomy and physiology and will carry out advanced first aid and resuscitation in all emergency situations. As a soldier, he is trained to use the fieldcraft and military skills required of an RAMC trained soldier in any active field unit anywhere in the world under hostilities. He has an ability to establish, manage and maintain a complete field hospital up to 200 beds in hostile and war-torn areas throughout the world.

He is trained to City and Guilds London Institute, Degree and Masters accreditation. Above all this an army OTT needs a very good sense of humour and fun with improvisational skills. Nothing fazes an OTT. This, as I have said, is just a very brief list of our training. We had to keep the surgeons and anaesthetist happy. Believe me, for some that was almost impossible. You needed a sense of humour to survive, and Pierre certainly did.

The OPERATING THEATRE TECHNICIAN - OTT

There is discipline in an OTT, you can see it when he walks,
There is honour in an OTT, you hear it when he talks.
There is courage in an OTT, you can see it in his eyes,
There is loyalty in an OTT that he will not compromise.
There is something in an OTT that makes him stand apart,
There is strength in an OTT that beats from his heart.
An OTT isn't a title any man can be hired to do,
An OTT is the soul of that man buried deep inside of you.
An OTT's job isn't finished after an 8 hour day or a 40 hour week,
An OTT is always an OTT, even while he sleeps.
An OTT serves his country first and his life is left behind,
An OTT has to sacrifice what comes first in a civilian's mind.

London in the Swinging Sixties

As a family unit, on arrival in the UK in December 1964, we lived in Amen Corner in Tooting Broadway, South London for some few months, until Mother and Father bought their own property in the Parsons Heath area of Colchester, Essex.

Here, Pop became a works foreman in a large coal distribution company, looking after their fleet of lorries. He also found enjoyable fishing on the east coast, around the area of Clacton on Sea, continuing his night fishing expeditions when the weather allowed him to do so.

They lived in Parsons Heath for their remaining days but, sadly, Pop had a massive unsuspected and untimely heart attack and died in 1974 at the young age of 57. Our mother continued to live there into her 70s.

Here in Colchester, my sister Marianna met and later married her husband while working as a secretary in his solicitor's office. He use to take her in his boat around the eastern coast nearby, where romance obviously struck. They had two daughters, Catriona and Emily, but later divorced. She has not remarried.

Life in London, especially in the swinging sixties, proved very exciting. We met up with old school chums from Dar who emigrated like us and lived in the Croydon area on a regular basis going to the city to enjoy the clubs and pubs.

I remember seeing the Rolling Stones playing a gig at the Wardour Club in the neon-clad vibrant part of Soho in London. We saw Sandie Shaw, of bare feet notoriety, at the Wimbledon Palais. Marianna saw the Beatles in action at the local Odeon cinema on Tooting Broadway high street, next to the tube station. Oh yes, those were the days.

Young brother Andy played in a rock band formed with other members and friends who had left Dar when we did and was in the music scene, playing in pubs and venues in and around Tooting, Colliers Wood, Wimbledon, Brixton and beyond. Pierre also formed his own band , with military colleagues in the army at Colchester. He was still playing their repertoire of Shadows numbers but had added a lot of new ones too.

So the music scene continued even after Dar es Salaam. These were great times. Music was in their blood.

It was here in London in 1965 in a music shop in Tooting Broadway high street that Andy and Pierre bought the guitar which is still much loved and treasured almost 50 years on. Andy vividly remembers, recalling the story that he saw a red and white Hank Marvin lookalike Fender Stratocaster guitar. It was a dream guitar, so he asked Mother to accompany him to the shop to buy it on a hire purchase agreement, as he was still not of age to do so himself. However, as they approached, the proprietor of the music shop, by the name of Mr Proctor, drew Andy aside to show him another guitar in the window display, one that had just arrived. Andy's heart just melted and knew instinctively this was the one for him.

It was the iconic and original Hank Marvin Burns signature guitar. Only just launched the previous year and built to Hank's specification and request by the famous Burns Guitars of London, it is now recognised some fifty years on as a collector's item. It had a beautiful white and turtle shell inlay inscribed with the signature of Hank Marvin of the Shadows, made from a single section of Canadian hard maple. Andy bought it for the princely sum of £165 pounds sterling. This was the flagship design model, and because of its originality and its provenance, this guitar would cost much more today and is sought by collectors all around the world.

On seeing Andy's guitar, Pierre went straight down to the shop and bought himself an identical one. These guitars would be their pride and joy, and some fifty years on, Andy still has goose pimples when playing his today. Some guitarists think of the USA as the only source of quality electric guitars and for the most part, they are correct. However, there are many who remember the superb range of guitars designed and made by Burns Guitars, a British company.

Way back in 1963, Jim Burns, the founder of the company, worked closely with Hank and Bruce Welch of The Shadows to design a guitar which would have the style, sound, and playability they required. Together they developed the 'Burns Marvin', a fine guitar, which Hank played on record, stage and screen from 1964 through to 1970, when, unfortunately, his guitars were stolen, never to be seen again, well not at least by Hank!

I still enjoy looking at the guitar and reminiscing whenever I visit Andy in Spain. Pierre and Andy would often have a jamming session with both their guitars. Other guitarists and musicians also marvel at this iconic guitar whenever it is played, emitting the lovely sound it producers. Andy has met the creator of the Burns Guitar and spoken enthusiastically about this famous instrument.

It was also here, in that very same music shop in Tooting Broadway, that Andy and Pierre met frequently and chatted about instruments and music with Errol Brown, who became famous as the lead vocalist of the popular and successful band Hot Chocolate, with hits such as "It Started With A Kiss" and "You Sexy Thing" as he once lived in the next London borough of Brixton.

Pierre took his beloved guitar everywhere he went around the world, finding friends and musicians to form bands. He enjoyed performing, whether it was entertaining the troops and their families or the general public. He had great charisma and personality, but above all, his art was strongly based on being a marvellous musician, singer and entertainer. He was a very animated character and would keep you talking for hours on end, as he was a tall story teller, and kept all amused.

Tony Sisley, a fellow OTT, colleague and family friend, recalls the time he was first invited to join the band while stationed in Hong Kong playing the keyboards and then later in Berlin. On hearing that Pierre was also there, even before commencing duty in the operating duty, he played a gig with the band. He spoke very highly and fondly of Pierre my brother.

They called themselves the Rough Diamond, and the band became very famous and popular throughout Hong Kong, even making television appearances and recordings. The band's popularity soared throughout Hong Kong, making many appearances in clubs and military establishments. Pierre recollects that a recording contract was offered, but because of military duties and restrictions, this had to be turned down.

The newspapers reports on the Rough Diamond group which appeared in daily newspaper cuttings included:

"Helping to bolster the few European groups are the "Rough Diamond", who were formed a few months ago. They are now ready to shake the foundations of Hong Kong rock music".

"Army group the Rough Diamond have made it to the top. This group at least tries to be different. They began by playing a mixture of blues and rock and have stuck to their guns to this day. Tony is the latest addition to the group, having just joined them some two months ago. From various reports, he is one of the most competent musicians on the local music scene, being a first class organist. At the moment the boys are waiting for the green light from RTV [local television studio].

"Lead guitarist Pierre Naya can play most of the instruments used in today's pop scene. Rough Diamond have been playing mostly at parties and service shows but have been seen at the In-Place a couple of times."

"A flood of votes for the Rough Diamond has pushed the popular services group up with the contenders in The Asian Group Section of the Star Pop Poll."

"Must be one of the favourites to capture the Beach Festival music competition."

This just shows the level of talent, fame and popularity they achieved while still servicemen in Hong Kong.

I am sure that if he had been spotted and managed by the right individual in the music industry, Pierre would have been very successful.

Pierre was renowned as a great communicator and storyteller, and could somehow remember countless jokes and ditties. He would be the life and soul of any party and would have you in stitches. He was a great mimic and had a remarkable grip on accents.

Later on, while in the Falklands War, all his comrades would say how he kept them amused, especially when things turned sour.

Pierre tells of one incident in Hong Kong when he survived a poolside incident while playing his guitar and entertaining the families. When the party was in full swing, with plenty of high jinks, frivolity, and drunkenness, he was thrown into the swimming pool while still attached to the electricity supply. How he was not electrocuted, I don't know. His guitar, however, was water damaged and began to rust in time. He got it fully refurbished some years on, by the original manufacturers in London, and subsequently sold it back to them.

CHAPTER ELEVEN

Following in Pierre's footsteps

I had decided that I wanted to follow the career path my brother Pierre had chosen. It was as simple as that. I wanted to follow in his footsteps. I always looked up to my elder brother with admiration. I began by enlisting at the South Norwood, London, Army Recruitment Office in February 1965. I pledged the next twenty-two years of my life to the Royal Army Medical Corps, just as Pierre had a year earlier.

I remember that day very clearly and proudly, because there I took my oath of allegiance to Her Majesty the Queen. It was an exciting moment tinged with anxiety, not unlike that experienced when we had left Dar es Salaam, but this time I had booked my voyage on a military future and was accepted to join the Royal Army Medical Corps (RAMC). I began my army career a few months after arriving in the UK at the age of seventeen. It was my dream and burning ambition to join my brother as an operating theatre technician in the British Army.

I was to join the Army and begin my basic military training at the

83

same centre as Pierre had done, at Keogh Barracks. I too wanted to become an Operating Theatre Technician (OTT) just like my brother, and I clearly remember the train journey from Waterloo train station in London to Ash Vale station. From there I made my way to Keogh Barracks near Aldershot, a large garrison town. It was early February 1965, a year in which the winter was particularly harsh, with severe snowfalls and chaos in the country due to the weather. I shivered continuously with cold, or was it fright?

As I was sitting in the train compartment feeling sorry for myself, lonely, very sad, anxious, and a little bit frightened, and feeling a bit homesick too, I struck up a conversation with a slightly older man. He must have been in his late thirties. It started with the usual exchange of polite questions. Then I added with great pride that I was joining the army and going to Keogh barracks to commence my basic training. He replied, "Oh yes, I am going there too".

My immediate thought was that at least I had met one person joining up like me, but that thought quickly vanished when he told me that he was not joining the army but going there to give himself up to the provost staff. He had been absent without leave for several years, forever on the run from the Military Police, and was now fed up with it all.

He had been conscripted into the services during the time of national service, which had not long finished, and had not taken well to it. The new form of recruitment to the services was taking place and I was part of that change. This chat with this unknown man horrified me and I wondered what sort of hell I was letting myself in for.

The army indoctrination began when you were given your never-ever-to-be-forgotten identity number. Forget this at your peril. Mine was 23997103 Private MRD Naya. This became etched into your memory. The cardinal sin was to forget it, so at every opportunity you were tested on it. It did not take long before this happened, when I attended my first drill instruction lesson on the parade square. I remember standing in total disarray on the square with the other new recruits for the very first time. I was determined to make an impression from day one, but it was a complete shambles.

From the distance of the square we could hear, see and recognise the spectre of an immaculately-dressed drill instructor marching smartly towards us. Everyone marched everywhere within the training depot – no walking.

His armoured boots made a loud thud on the drill square with every step he took. His pace quickening as he approached the drill square, his kingdom. His pace stick was under one armpit, with the other hand swinging, perfectly synchronised with his steps. His boots were shining like glass. Hat peak lowered, so you could barely see his eyes. He was the epitome of a drill pig. He was here to psyche you out, and break you if possible.

We got into some sort of formation as he came round individually, shouting his request at each of us in turn for our number, rank and name. We were all quaking in our boots. Then he came to me, his face not more than six inches away from mine. I already knew that you never looked into a drill instructor's eyes but straight ahead, no matter what. Pierre did tell me what to expect, but to experience it yourself is something else.

He yelled at me, with droplets of spit splattering my face and in a fierce blood chilling roar, "Name? What's your f...ing name?"

I was about to wee my pants with fright. "23997103 Pte Naya, sir" I tried to shout, but the words barely came out.

"For f...k's, sake, not another f...ing Naya" he replied. In the relief of that moment, I think I did wet my pants. He had remembered Pierre from the previous year. "Where the f...ing hell is he now?" he bellowed, still spitting in my face as he was so close. I managed to reply, "He is in Colchester, sir".

"Best place for him", he answered, "What did he do wrong?"

"No sir, he is not in the military correction wing there. He's in the military hospital doing his training."

He moved along the line. Phew! What a bastard.

His name was Chas Debues, and I later found he had been an OTT himself earlier in his service. What a small world. I would buy him a beer today if he was still around, but sadly, he has passed away. I often recall this story to Pierre, and we would enjoy reminiscing about this period in our lives. Of course Pierre would mimic, the bark of the drill sergeant to a tee.

I recall doing the routine camp guard duty and walking round the barrack grounds checking buildings with just the regulation wooden truncheon and visiting what was rumoured to be the haunted Mytchett House and Camp Z. It was where the infamous Rudolf Hess, Hitler's deputy, was imprisoned during 1941, after being transferred from the Tower of London. This was the scene of one of his failed suicide attempts. He had thrown himself off one of the balconies, only to land on a sentry parading down below. This place gave us all the creeps, with tales of weird happenings, sounds and creepiness, so we tried to keep away from this area as much as possible.

In later years, Hess did commit suicide. The sole inmate of Spandau Prison, in Berlin, he was found in the gardens with a wire flex round his neck. He was taken to the British Military hospital in Berlin and pronounced dead at the age of ninety three.

The next sixteen weeks disappeared in a blur. Military pay, in the early sixties, was five guineas, of which I saved three, in the Post Office savings account we were encouraged to open.

During this time, I met Phil Olive, who was also a recruit like me. As well as later being my best man at my wedding, our paths subsequently crossed several times during our military service, both in the UK and West Germany. Our friendship survived the upheavals and we have remained very good friends and meet up at our OTT reunions.

After completing my initial basic training it was the normal practice to be interviewed by the Technical Training Officer. In my case, this was a certain Lt. Col. Tennuci, RAMC. I had enlisted with the clear intention of following Pierre's lead the year before to train as an OTT, but I was initially devastated when he told me that I could not do so. Apparently there was a surplus of OTTs in the Corps and there was no further requirement at that stage. Pierre was distraught about the news, as I would not be joining him. So I went instead into the nurse training stream, as I knew that the overstaffing was only a temporary issue. Consequently I am dual trained, which has stood me well in future employment opportunities since leaving the army.

I was posted to Tidworth Military Hospital in Wiltshire for the next seven years and completed my nurse training before being given the opportunity to begin my Operating Theatre Technician, or OTT, training. I achieved my goal, just as I had planned. That I did so in this slightly roundabout way accounts for the length of this, my very first posting. During this period I married my first wife and had two lovely daughters, both born in the military hospital maternity wing in Tidworth. Rachel was born in 1970 and Rebecca in 1971. Both now live in Hereford and have their own families.

With his innate luck Pierre, in 1970, found himself posted to the military hospital in Hong Kong for the first of his two tours there. Lucky devil! Every serving soldier dearly wanted the exotic overseas posting, especially one often described as the jewel of the Far East.

By that time, Pierre had married Nina, and both were avid ten pin bowlers. Just how good a pair they were was proved by the number of bowling competitions and trophies they won while on that posting. He always had a great eye.

Pay was low in those days and it was a real struggle for us to bring up our two children. It must have been worse for Nina and Pierre with four young children. Our first married quarter was in a Coronation Street-style house in Tidworth. They were classed as sub-standard, yet still rented out to us by the Army. They were pulled down a few years later and we were given a more modern and up-to-date house in the Sidbury Close married quarters area. It meant moving about two miles away, and moving home with two small children, as with other matters, had to be carefully budgeted. The memories of how we transferred all our belongings on the many return journeys needed, pushing my daughters' overloaded, second hand silver cross pram, are both painful and embarrassing.

After serving seven years in Tidworth I felt like a fixture there, but I desperately wanted to move on to an oversees posting. At that time we had several far-flung military hospitals in Singapore, Hong Kong and Cyprus. I applied for a transfer, saw the personnel officer, was interviewed, and finally applied for Singapore. No chance. In typically perverse military fashion, I was posted to Cyprus instead. After seven years, I really should have learned how to get this right. They never give you the posting you request.

So, in 1972, I was posted to the British Military Hospital in Cyprus with my family. It was a joy to receive an overseas posting with all the perks that went with it, like extra overseas allowance and duty free perks. I bought my first motor car, a Datsun Cherry, for the sum of £650 Cypriot pounds. At last I was beginning to enjoy life in the Army.

I arrived just in time to experience the unrest in the island which resulted in the 1974 invasion and its subsequent demarcation. Today, this beautiful island still lies divided into the Turkish and Greek zones.

The politics of Cyprus evolved from the shadow of the dominant figure of Archbishop and President Makarios, who embodied the struggle for independence from Britain and *enosis*, the political union of Cyprus with Greece. After independence was achieved without enosis, Makarios's own thinking changed and Cypriot politics struggled to come to terms with its own ghost, the union of Greece and Cyprus. In July 1974,the military junta in Athens sponsored a coup led by extremist Greek Cypriots against the government of President Makarios, citing his alleged pro-communist leanings and his perceived abandonment of enosis. The Greek Cypriot coup was aimed at uniting Cyprus with mainland Greece. The situation was controlled, but the island remains divided with the potential that presents.

Having two similarly qualified Nayas in the same Corps was bound at some stage to create the confusion which was to dog my service life. It first occurred when I was summoned to the personnel office to see the officer in charge, a Major. This was very unusual and I had no idea why he might have sent for me. It usually meant you were in some sort of trouble and I feared for my future.

I was briskly marched into the office by The Regimental Sergeant Major, left, right, left, right, left, right, HALT! I stood smartly at attention in front of his desk. I was correctly dressed in uniform. He was reading from a piece of paper he held in one hand as he put out his right hand to shake mine.

Smiling all the while, he said, "Congratulations, you have been promoted to Lance Corporal, Private Naya".

I breathed a sigh of relief and elation as he handed me the piece of paper from the records office in the UK to read. My relief turned to concern as I looked at it. He noticed something was wrong by the expression on my face. I had to point out that this paper, in fact, was not for me, but for my brother Pierre. It was he who had been promoted, which the personnel officer should have checked by referring to the army number on it. It was an embarrassing experience for both of us and I was dismissed with apologies. Although initially disappointed that the promotion was not mine, I was over the moon for my brother Pierre.

Even without frequent direct communication between us in different parts of the world, somehow, usually via the grapevine, we always found out what each other was doing. The thought that Pierre was keeping a filial eye on me induced in me the feeling that I was in his shadow, and that my brother was looking out for me. Pierre at this time was on his first of two tours of service in Hong Kong at the operating theatres of the military hospital there.

While in Cyprus I was seconded for a short period to reinforce the field hospital team we had in Salala in the state of Oman. I was in my early twenties by then. Travelling to Oman, from Cyprus, leaving on New Year's Eve, we had a very uncomfortable thirteen-hour flight on a Hercules troop transporter aircraft of the Royal Air Force to the Oman to undertake my first posting to an active war zone. I was very anxious about going to a theatre of war miles away from my wife and two children in Cyprus.

I have very little to show for that posting, for my stay there was too short even for me to qualify for a general service medal. What I did leave with, however, was a new-found and immense respect for the courage and dedication of people committed to military action, especially those of the Special Air Service (SAS).

There was an active war going on in which British forces of the SAS were in station, as the so called British Army Training Team, helping the Sultan of Oman to repulse the rebels high in the rough mountain terrain. This was a covert campaign that the British government obviously supported, but we could not divulge where we were, although it was reported in UK newspapers.

The famous battle of Mirbat took place in July 1972. Though killed in action, Sgt Labalaba, one of the SAS soldiers, displayed remarkable bravery by single-handedly operating the 25-pounder gun, a weapon normally requiring four to six soldiers to operate. Labalaba's heroism was a key factor in halting the Adoos' vicious assault on the emplacement of the SAS, allowing time for reinforcements to arrive. Labalaba was awarded a posthumous mention in dispatches for his actions in the Battle of Mirbat, though some of his comrades have since campaigned for him to be awarded the more prestigious Victoria Cross. I hope in time they will succeed in their quest for rightful recognition for this brave and heroic soldier. I salute and honour the brave lads of the SAS and the soldiers of Pakistan and Oman who were also caught up in their heroic stand that day.

My unit was located around 25 kilometres from Mirbat. We were a small one-team field surgical hospital, doing a great job for the army by treating mainly civilians from far and wide. A hearts and minds programme really, and it gave me the opportunity to catch up with many familiar faces.

In October 1974, while serving in Cyprus, I had the terrible news from our mother living in Colchester that our beloved Pop had passed away from a severe heart attack at the age of 57. It happened without warning and that day became and remains one of the saddest of my life. He had taught us well and showed us a way of life and its understanding that we, his family, treasure to this day. The Army immediately got me a compassionate flight back home to attend his funeral.

There was much to do while in Cyprus besides my medical duties. I continued to enjoy my football and represented the army in athletics. Matches and events were usually against the Royal Air Force, and my best races were the short sprint events.

Pierre was just as fast as me - our speed had been honed as teenagers in Dar es Salaam, when we needed to be fast enough to escape immediate retribution for our misdemeanours. If just a little bored and the opportunity arose, we might creep up on a sleeping African night-watchman who had been employed to guard a particular shop, bank or other premises in the high street against loutish behaviour such as we were about to display by waking him up with a gentle kick. His annoyed response was instant as he gave chase, but we knew that these watchmen were generally older men so that we did not have to be very fast, except over the first fifty yards or so. I sometimes dread to think what would have happened if we had been caught, but we gave ourselves no chance to find out.

I represented the hospital in Cyprus in one special event with a highly coveted trophy. This was the annual fifteen-mile relay road race, held from Ayios Nikolaos to Dhekelia, called the Dhekelia Dash. Each of the fifteen men stationed a mile apart had to run the mile, and at each handover your team-mate had to drink a pint of beer before he was allowed to set off with the baton in hand. Yes it was dreadful following the man in front spewing beer as he ran, but what great fun. You had to overtake quickly, or else.

We won the trophy three times. We must have been able to hold our beer better than others. Oh the fitness of youth!

In later years, when this event became very competitive, beer drinking was banned. The need for speed required a positive approach to training and the hospital team took their training very seriously and trained hard.

I do remember, during training over a measured mile, being given the task, and honour, of carrying the stop watch. We all started off at the start line together and I had to run as fast as possible to stand at the finish line and count the rest of the runners in, shouting out their times. That's how fit I was. My time over the mile back then was four minutes and seventeen seconds. Just shows what fear of a night-watchman's stick can do.

During the next twenty-three years of my army career, I was posted to military hospitals in Hong Kong, Nepal, Cyprus, and various other units in West Germany and the United Kingdom, serving in operating theatres, all the while providing support to senior medical staff and ready to be deployed to trouble spots around the world wherever and whenever needed.

Travels with the RAMC

Pierre and I, although identically qualified, were never posted together in the same unit. I don't think anyone could put up with the two Nayas together, leave alone two brothers. However, as a closely-knit group of OTTs, we often made the same friends at different times and places.

People would continually ask me about my brother, where he was and how his wife and children were. Invariably they would ask if he was still playing the guitar and want news of his band.

In 1976 I was posted to the British Military Hospital at Rinteln, a beautiful, spotlessly-clean town in a rural area of West Germany on the river Wesser about 100km south of Bremen. There I met and married my wife Barbara, who was a nurse in the Queen Alexandra's Royal Army Nursing Corp. I remember having to write to the hospital matron to ask her permission for me to marry one of her soldiers. Luckily for me she agreed.

Soon after our marriage, the merry-go-round of postings and moving on to other military hospitals continued. I found myself in another West German town, Iserlohn, which is about 130 km from Rinteln, after a brief tour back at our training school at Aldershot.

Our son was born in January 1984 at the maternity wing in the military hospital at Munster, West Germany and, of course, we named him after my late father, Rene.

Barbara continued to serve as a nurse until the birth of Rene, completing twelve years' service in the Military Nursing Corps with the rank of Sergeant.

As both Pierre's career and mine progressed, we met and served with many memorable colleagues. At the military hospital in Iserlohn I served with a certain Major Amit Banerjee. He was an Indian anaesthetist. What a popular, charismatic, kind and gentle man he was. One odd thing about him was that while he had the style and looked the part on the cricket pitch, he couldn't play to save his life.

Pierre had yet to meet and work with this anaesthetist, by then a consultant. Pierre was destined to have to wait until they both found themselves in a very demanding wartime condition in the Falklands War, working on the same field surgical team operating on casualties.

I have learned over the years that some of the incidents that people remember for a very long time were, and possible still are, personally embarrassing. One such occurred during one of my several spells working at our OTT training school theatres at the Cambridge Military Hospital in Aldershot in the late 70s. One night I was on call and found myself in the operating theatre side by side with a very senior technician, with many more years of experience than I had. He was a chap called Bill H, a Cockney character with a reputation for straight talking, never one to mince his words.

During the operation the sister asked if the diathermy machine, which we both happened to be leaning on at the time, could be switched on. We were standing side by side, inches from the surgeon, patient and operation site. This meant that both of us would have to move to concur with her request. Without hesitation he said, "Ah, f.... off" in a pissed-off tone. I knew that he had been concentrating and was annoyed by the interruption, but nevertheless I was shocked by his reaction, and so too were the operating team. I said sheepishly, "It's all right Bill, I will do it".

I was thoroughly embarrassed. It was all over in a moment, but those few seconds have lingered with me. We meet occasionally at our OTT Reunions and this story nearly always crops up. Bill is one of those characters who makes an instant impact, and is widely known and respected by all, including experienced high-ranking surgeons. Even retirement from the NHS has not done much to smooth the edges, and he is still very direct. Being an old and respected soldier of many years service, and also one who was demoted for misdemeanours, he did not care too much about the way he addressed people and did not tolerate fools gladly. He should have attained a higher ranking status of sergeant than he did.

Here at the Cambridge Military Hospital I was to meet a then young surgeon, Captain Jim Ryan. What a gentleman and friend he turned out to be, a brilliant, prolific and very hard-working military surgeon. He later became Professor of Military Surgery for the army. He also became a friend to both Pierre and myself.

Jim Ryan was the type of man and surgeon who both Pierre and I instinctively respected. We would follow and work for him under any conditions anywhere in the world. He was articulate and kind, with a sense of humour, and he genuinely cared for the men who worked under him.

Other, less experienced, military surgeons would start demanding instruments at the operating table in a manner they might use in a large NHS theatre environment. That was not Jim Ryan's way. With his trust, you were also a professional whose recommendations and judgements he would not question. If you did not have the particular instrument he preferred, he would accept your word without question and get around the problem another way. This was the right approach, especially in remote parts of the world. His confidence radiated to all the team around him and provided great motivation to others. A great man, great surgeon and great friend.

Pierre was to meet and work with Jim Ryan under very different conditions in 1982, but I was to cross his path again in the British Military Hospital in Nepal in the late 80s,where we had a small 70-bedded hospital. We looked after the British Gurkha regiment and their families, who were recruited from the foothills of the lush Himalaya Mountain range.

This hospital lies 45 miles north of the Indian border in East Nepal, nestling at the foot of the Sangure Ridge. This marks the beginning of the foothills of the Himalayas. On a clear day from the top of the ridge, Mount Everest is visible eighty miles away to the north.

The hospital sits in the idyllic surroundings of the British Cantonment of Dharan, two square miles of England which was transplanted into the forest in the early sixties. Outside this is the more primitive country of Nepal, with few of the basic amenities we take for granted in the rest of the world, such as drinking water, regular electricity and adequate sanitation. The cantonment has all these things, along with a swimming pool that doubles as an emergency water supply, stables, a nine-hole golf course with a long par five hole that doubles as an emergency landing strip for light aircraft. The greens were properly prepared with good drainage to handle the monsoon season.

I took my first steps here in learning the gentle art of golf. We had a well-stocked clubhouse and ran many golfing tournaments. Tuitions was provided by the resident Indian golf professional. The caddies were often low handicapped golfers themselves and would accompany you for a few rupees per round. It was only later that we found they would have side bets on our games and they were not above giving your ball a nudge with one of their flip-flops to create a better lie if your ball was in the rough. It livened up the game for them too. What rascals they were!

Barbara would occupy herself by doing voluntary work in our local British Forces Broadcasting Station (BFBS), by introducing and playing tapes and records from London and Hong Kong. It was lovely to hear her voice on the radio, which was piped to every single quarter on the cantonment. She clearly had a good grasp of the workings on the central console, with its complex of dials, sliders and switches.

I was, by then, the senior staff sergeant in charge of the operating theatres, working with five local civilian technicians. We looked after the acute medical needs of local civilians and were responsible for a wide range of surgical procedures that they might require too, as they had no access to medical facilities other than the hospital.

All this was under the auspices of Colonel Jim Ryan, who was not to know that after working with Pierre in extremely inhospitable war conditions in the South Atlantic a few years earlier, he was destined to renew an association a few years later with another, the author, in much more pleasant circumstances, some 8,800 miles from the Falklands. The salt cellar approach the army appeared to use to allocate its postings had shaken well that day when ours coincided.

There was a time when it was said that the sun never set on the British Empire. By the time of the Falklands campaign, this was no longer true. Most of the colonies had achieved independence, many retaining their old contacts through the Commonwealth that the renamed Empire had become. Even though fixed overseas bases were slowly closing, the scale of service operations remained worldwide, but the speed of communications and transport had made the world a much smaller place.

Here we operated only on two days of the week, from seven in the morning to early evening. The time we had to operate was restricted by often inadequate supplies we had in stock because the King of Nepal had placed restrictions on what medical stores could be imported into his country. It seemed perverse of him to have done so when we were providing a badly-needed service to his people. It still rankles when I think about it.

This was the very same king who was murdered some years later by one of his own sons in a drugs and alcohol-induced rage. In the process he wiped out the whole of the royal family by shooting them in cold blood in the Royal Palace in Kathmandu, the capital.

As we had only one complete surgical team, the operating sessions were extremely tiring. The operating list would consist of twenty or so patients, all of whom would be very acute cases. They might have walked for three days to get to the hospital from their homes high in the hills and valleys. We witnessed hernias so large that the patient had to be brought to us in a wheelbarrow, as that was the only way that they could be moved.

Our living quarter was a colonial style whitewashed bungalow. What I found very difficult to come to terms with was the employment of its domestic staff. You inherited not just the married quarter from your predecessor, but the civilian domestic Nepalese staff who lived in their own little one-roomed house, attached to the main house. You also inherited the responsibility not only of paying their wages, but generally looking after their welfare. Getting used to this scenario brought back memories of Dar es Salaam where our parents also had the task of looking after the staff they employed there.

We had a gardener called Jaghdar Persaud, and an Ayah, a Nepalese lady named Sheba, who generally looked after our home, washing, cleaning, tidying and ironing. Some others had a cook as well, but we didn't. These local civilian Nepalese staff were very loyal and enjoyed being employed by us British troops. It provided them with work and an income and you looked after them as part of your extended family.

While I was serving here in this beautiful location, Her Majesty The Queen Elizabeth and His Royal Highness The Prince Phillip, Duke of Edinburgh, paid us a visit on 20th February, 1986. I received an invitation letter stating that the British Ambassador had been commanded by the Queen to invite me to a reception at the British Embassy in Kathmandu at 12 noon. My junior, our theatre sister, also desperately wanting to see the Queen. Despite my longing to see her too, someone had to stay back in the cantonment to cover any emergencies. So she went to Kathmandu and I stayed behind to provide emergency medical cover for the landing of the helicopter bringing Prince Phillip to a nearby sports field. It was a very nervous time for me, as all I had was a trauma bag and the task of providing medical cover for this important VIP.

I was informed that the second helicopter to land carried the royal blood in case of a disaster. Apparently that's the arrangement when the Royals visit locations around the world. I felt that it was a great honour to be invited, and to this day, I have that invitation displayed with pride in my home.

Very sadly, the hospital closed in 1989, soon after I had left for Hong Kong. Yet again, a fantastic posting for the family.

One of my last postings in the forces was to the military hospital in Hong Kong where Pierre also served many years previously. I worked with an army major surgeon by the name of David Jackson, who had been the lead surgeon for Pierre's team in 1982 in the Falklands War. It is how extraordinary how fate brings people together. The more we travel, the smaller the world appears to become. They say that mountains don't meet, but people do. I find that to be very true in life.

One of the military recreational places put aside for the British forces at that time was a tiny military island called Stonecutters Island.

This was just off Kowloon City and Hong Kong island, and the only way to get there was by a special military ferry, taking twenty to thirty minutes. The ferry plied back and forth frequently, carrying supplies, families, and other personnel to and from the island. The idea was to give personnel some respite from the hustle and bustle of Hong Kong city. This particular island was essentially a British Forces ammunition depot. It had been one for many years, including World War Two. Then, it was deliberately infested with many deadly poisonous snakes to deter intruders, so access to all parts were severely restricted.

The island also had a military firing range, where we held our annual compulsory weapons training, firing at wooden targets painted as German soldiers.

It was during this posting that I arranged for my daughters and in-laws to holiday with us. My in-laws are Yorkshire people born and bred. I remember one particular outing to the bright lights of the city when we visited the area of Kowloon called Tsim Sha Tsui, on the mainland. This area is full of restaurants and bars, some legal, others not. There were strip clubs, gay clubs, jazz clubs, in fact anything or any type you wanted. To set the scene, all you need to know that the normal price for a San Miguel beer is five HK dollars.

I decided to take them to a bar called Bottoms Up which has become iconic to James Bond aficionados. This bar was used in the film *The Man With The Golden Gun*, which was filmed there in 1974. It featured Roger Moore as Bond in the downstairs mirror-clad bar. Here you were seated at round tables with topless waitresses of all nationalities. Very attractive they were too! I chose to sit with the English one. It was also my father-in-law's turn to buy the beers. The faces of my in-laws were a picture to behold when the beers arrived! One does not see these goings-on in the pubs of Whitby where they lived.

When the time came to pay for the one round we had had, my father-in-law took the bill and his face fell a mile when he had taken a few seconds to work out the price of the beers. It was fifty Hong Kong dollars per beer. "You're having a laugh" were the only words he could find as he quickly passed me the bill. "You can pay for this, my lad".

Fortunately, I knew what the prices were likely to be as we had been there a few times before, after regimental dinners when slightly worse for wear.

"Ee by gum!" he said. "Wait till I tell my mates at the Conservative Club in Whitby about this."

Playing golf in the new territories was like living in a different world. As we were in the army, this allowed us the privilege of being society members of Fanlings Royal Hong Kong Golf Club, with its millionaire clientele.

We were now mixing with the best of high society in this renowned club. However, battered army Land Rovers parked next to the immaculate Rolls Royce did nothing to improve the mood of the chauffeur. There was a two-year waiting list to join this exclusive club, which had three championship golf courses and held world-class events in the golfing calendar. The clubhouse was a study in class and opulence, and the changing rooms all had warmed high-class towels, individual lockers and attendees to meet your needs.

It would sometimes give us the jitters as we rubbed shoulders with the mega-rich. We could but tell ourselves that we were all equal once we were on the greens, where the ability to play took priority over style, fame and fortune.

All the time Pierre was never far from my thoughts. I tried to imagine his band playing at gigs around the city of Hong Kong, the adoration of fans, and the wonderful talent he had playing his much beloved Hank Marvin Burns guitar.

CHAPTER THIRTEEN

Sailing for the South Atlantic

In March 1982, Pierre, now a senior sergeant and a very experienced operating theatre technician and soldier, was posted from the Cambridge Military Hospital in Aldershot to 2 Field Hospital. This very small regular army unit was just round the corner from the Cambridge hospital and OTT training school, where Pierre was stationed, teaching the young trainees.

In normal times, the establishment strength of this unit is a cadre of three officers and 38 soldiers. These alone are insufficient to staff a hospital, so in a war situation this increases to 48 officers and some 140 soldiers, all of whom are Royal Army Medical Corps personnel, highly trained in different specialities to run and staff a 200-bed field hospital.

The field hospital's primary role is to train for war in a European context, but it also has a secondary role to be prepared for any disaster or situation on a worldwide basis. It is permanently ready to move at seven days' notice, for any eventuality.

The members of the cadre alone are insufficient to staff a hospital,

103

so nominated suitable qualified officers with medical, dental and nursing experience together with servicemen and servicewomen from hospitals and other medical units throughout the country are nominated as potential reinforcements for a period of time at short notice, to bring the cadre up to full strength. These reinforcements are divided into Category One and Category Two. Category One personnel include a surgical team and together with the cadre, provide the staff for a 50-bed hospital. The addition of Category Two personnel enables the hospital to expand to accommodate a 100-bed unit with two surgical teams. The option exists to establish a full 200-bed hospital with four surgical teams, but it would only be called upon in the event of full mobilisation.

So, in 1982, as Pierre was sent to 2 Field Hospital, I was posted from the Queen Elizabeth Military Hospital in Woolwich London to replace him in Aldershot. At long last we were in the same place, although not in the same unit.

The sun now had its shadow. As brothers, although I feel that we had the same work ethic, our characters were as different as chalk and cheese. Pierre had a huge personality and charisma. He was the spark of much humour among his colleagues. He had an extremely mischievous streak which put life and soul into any gathering. This was his social front, underneath which he was made of much sterner stuff, making him both well liked and very well respected. He had nerves of steel and an abundance of energy and determination.

One of his ploys was to wet both hands, creep up behind an unsuspecting colleague and pretend to sneeze, at the same time shaking his wet hands at the neck of his victim. The instant annoyance and disgust on their faces always changed quickly to embarrassed laughter as they realised that they had been caught by Pierre yet again. Why no one tore him limb from limb was all down to his aura.

It was in Aldershot that Pierre introduced me to wine making. It was a favourite hobby of his, among other things like art and painting, at which he excelled. He produced lovely pictures and portraits, but, come party time, he would also bake cakes and make beautiful cake decorations, and cook good food for all. He rounded it off by brewing some lovely red and white wine, and it was fun consuming a bottle or two with him.

Within a few weeks the situation in the Falklands had become clearer and our military preparations more determined after the Argentines had occupied them under the rule of General Galtieri. It was Pierre's destiny to participate and play a major role in this event.

I remember subsequently feeling quite selfish about a small, in itself, event on the evening of the 11th May 1982, when he was preparing to join his unit, being sent as part of the task force to the Falklands on the following day. I rang him at home, and asked why my red wine, which we had both started, had not begun fermenting. He assured me with his usual calmness that it would start to do so very soon and that I was to stop fretting. He asked me not to drink it all and save some for him, when, and not if, he returned.

It did start fermenting a few days later. The following day he and his unit left Aldershot for Southampton to join the luxury but now converted passenger liner Queen Elizabeth 2 to prepare to sail south to war.

At the end of April 1982, QE2 was returning to her homeport of Southampton, England, after making her transatlantic voyage from the USA. The ship's company was aware that a number of British-flag ships, including the popular P&O cruise ship Canberra, had been commandeered by the British Government, but no one seriously expected QE2 to be requisitioned. The ship was the largest, most luxurious and fastest passenger ship in service, and the only one still making regular scheduled transatlantic crossings. She had been constructed during the late 1960s. She cost nearly £30 million and was by far the most famous ship in the world.

Meanwhile, at a meeting at the Prime Minister's country residence, Margaret Thatcher was advised that the QE2 was required to transport the next wave of troops to the Falklands. She asked whether it was really necessary or advisable to use this great ship and put so many people in it, but as soon as she was told that it was necessary to get them to the Falklands in time, she gave her permission.

As the QE2 neared England, she began to pick up commercial radio broadcasts that said she had been requisitioned. After confirming these reports with Cunard's shoreside offices, the Captain made a public announcement that the ship would be leaving service following passenger disembarkation the next day. Approximately 1,000 officers and crew members volunteered to accompany QE2 into the war zone. Out of these, 650 were selected, including 33 women.

After disembarking the passengers, work began to transform the QE2. Artwork, silver, furniture, and casino equipment were taken ashore for storage. Wooden panels were laid down to protect the carpets from the soldiers' boots. Although the troops would not be packed in as they had been during World War II on the Queen Mary, which carried as many as 16,000 soldiers, the plan was to take 3,000 soldiers on, roughly 1,000 more people than her maximum peacetime passenger capacity.

In addition, military communications equipment was brought onboard and a secure communications centre was constructed. Tons of military stores and cargo were brought on, including vehicles, jet fuel and ammunition. Since there was more than would fit in the hold, some supplies, including ammunition, were stored on the open deck near the funnel.

The most significant alteration came because the military wanted to use QE2 not just as a troopship, but as a helicopter carrier as well. Since the ship is 963 feet long and has plenty of open deck space, this did not seem to be much of a problem.

The solution was to build two heliports. The smaller one would be built forward of the superstructure on a platform extending over the capstans. The second platform would be built aft, resting on a series of girders that would be anchored in the structures that supported the weight of the ship's two outdoor swimming pools. However, since QE2's open decks aft were built in a series of terraces, part of the superstructure had to be cut away in order to create an expanse large enough to meet the military's requirements.

Once the alterations were completed, the ship embarked the troops, consisting primarily of the Fifth Infantry Brigade, which comprised battalions from the Scots Guards, the Welsh Guards and the Queen's Own Gurkha Rifles. The plan was that these units would be the main British invasion force, following up on initial landings made by the Royal Marine Commandos and troops from the Parachute Regiment, who were already en route down south. Considering that Britain's plans were built around these troops, it is clear that much depended upon QE2. Indeed, if she had been lost, it is difficult to see how Britain could have prevailed.

Arriving at Southampton docks Pierre and the rest of 55 Field Surgical Team could see the imposing shape of the QE2 before them. There were thousands of well-wishers all along the shore and dock area bidding farewell to the troops. The massed bands of the Household Calvary were playing *Men of Harlech*, then *Scotland the Brave*. Eventually they were told to board to the tune of "Here's a health to Her Majesty", our RAMC regimental quick march.

Then on boarding, Pierre told us later, what a letdown. All the fixtures and fittings and silverware had been removed - no carpets, no pictures, no nothing. The welders were still working at the blunt end, sparks flying and smoke rising.

They were all told to amass on the port side deck for leaving harbour, combats and berets to be worn. There was cheering and waving to love ones. Their feelings were tinged with sadness at going to war, wondering if some of them would not return.

The massive turbines were humming, making the decking tremble, and several tugs and other small crafts were all around. As the ship cleared the mole, hundreds, even thousands, of little ships followed. There were many helicopters in the air as well and then they became aware of the thousands of people standing on the shores, waving union jacks and cheering. In good old British squaddies' humour, someone started singing "We're all going on a summer holiday", and this was soon taken up by the lads and became their adopted song.

The ship moved slowly down Southampton Water, surrounded by tugs. QE2 was going slowly because she could not go any faster. During the previous transatlantic voyage, one of the ship's boilers had been taken down for routine maintenance. Now one of the other boilers had sprung a massive leak. As a result, the ship had only one working boiler and could only manage seven knots, a speed at which the ship was difficult to control. Thus, the tugs surrounding the ship were not ceremonial escorts but were there to help manoeuvre and propel the giant ship. Once out of sight of land, QE2 anchored and repair work commenced. In the end, the problem turned out to be a valve that had been left in the wrong position. The repair work took some 12 hours. Now that QE2 was capable of attaining her service speed, she headed out to sea, leaving the third boiler to be repaired en route.

Then army life at sea began in earnest. No one was allowed on deck except when it was your unit's scheduled time for physical training, running around the decks.

The fitness of Major Banerjee, who was on Pierre's team as the anaesthetist, impressed the instructor. He remarked on how fit he looked. That was because the crafty major used to sneak through the centre of the ship and wait to join the end of the line trailing around.

There were endless rounds of setting up the Field Surgical Team's equipment against the stop watch, what to do if you lose kit, half of the kit, quarter of the kit etc. Aircraft recognition proved very useful later, studying maps and attending briefings on the Falklands, being updated on the military situation, 'O' groups, lifeboat drill, firing live rounds off the stern at black rubbish bags thrown into the sea as targets.

The first leg of QE2's voyage was marked by regimental dinners and evening entertainment by the various regimental bands. Officers were assigned to eat in the luxury Queens Grill restaurant, while senior NCOs had to make do with the slightly less sumptuous Princess Grill. Other ranks used the ship's two large dining rooms.

The QE2 switched off her stabiliser so she could go faster, causing her to roll and pitch more. They had no idea that they were being followed by one of our submarines for cover, or watched by Russian trawlers.

The Fifth Infantry Brigade had just completed training exercises in the Welsh mountains, as this terrain was deemed most similar to the Falklands. To maintain their edge, the troops continued to exercise during their weeks on board the QE2. Soldiers running in full combat gear around the one-fifth mile jogging track on the Boat Deck, caused the caulking to protrude from between the teak planks.

The Gurkhas were especially serious about staying fit. Starting at the bottom of "A" Stairway, one soldier would climb on the back of another, who would then run up eight decks. To simulate conditions if the ship lost power and was in darkness, the runners were blindfolded.

The first leg ended when the ship arrived in Freetown, Sierra Leone, to take on fuel and water. Little effort had been made so far to keep the ship's movements secret, and the ship had been observed by a Soviet spy trawler. After leaving Freetown, however, the ship's radar was turned off, electronic silence was observed and the ship was blacked out at night. With hundreds of portholes and large picture windows, achieving a full blackout was impossible without painting the windows black, so black garbage bag plastic was taped over them. While this arrangement blocked the light, the plastic caused a greenhouse effect which severely taxed the ship's air conditioning as she traversed the tropics.

Moving down south, the heat of the tropics was replaced by the onset of the South Atlantic winter. Lookouts were placed on the bridge wings and near the funnel as a precaution against icebergs. All watertight doors were shut. The ship's officers and the naval authorities agreed to risk giving away the ship's location by turning on the radar. The radar sweep showed over 100 icebergs in the vicinity. Most were small, but others were miles long and hundreds of feet high. All night the ship weaved through the deadly ice.

I would like to share with the readers excerpts from some of Pierre's personal letters he wrote to his wife Nina. I am indebted to Nina for her permission to use them. These are his own words, the first of which he wrote on the 16th May 1982, four days after sailing for the Falklands.

My darling Pomme,

I hope you are well and looking after yourself, as for me I am fine. Did you see me on TV when we set off? I don't suppose you did, never mind. There were so many lads on board that we had to fight for a space to wave from. Eventually I ended up on the second deck below the lifeboats, towards the back of the boat.

As we pulled out of Southampton I waved to the news helicopters from the end of the ship, right at the back. I am sharing a room with 3 other sergeants, one is Cleverly Parker from Woolwich who is in charge of the second FST, I am in charge of the 1st.

We are now 1270 miles from Freetown on the west coast of Africa, where we are to stop for water and fuel. They won't post our letters from there, because there are complaints that the mail is being held up there. So we will have a mail collection and delivery from the Ascension Islands when we leave Freetown. We are not allowed off the ship when we get there.

We do a lot of PT and running round the ship every day for an hour. We also do a lot of weapon and military training, as well as training on how to use our FST. We have set up one FST at the front of the ship below the dining area, and one at the back of the ship, near the helicopter pad.

We are in room 2138 on deck two. Number seven deck is below the water line. We are only allowed to use this type of letter paper, as its freepost.

We are allowed £15 a week from our pay, we just sign a ledger, and its stopped from our pay automatically.

The ship's very big, with shops and various bars and grills, which have been turned into messes for Officers, SNCOs and Juniors, plus crew.

So far have not spent much money because essentials are so cheap on board. Cigs 27p a packet, spirits 15p a tot, beer 25p a can. I am getting fitter by the day. Food is very good and us SNCOs have waiter service in the lounge.

The entire ship has been covered in hardboard and canvas on all the carpets and stairways, and it's stripped of all its luxury items, but you can still tell she is really the Queen of The Merchant Navy fleet.

So darling don't send me any money or cigs.

I have been put in charge of a life raft and 25 men, what a responsibility eh! Give my love to all at home and pray that we are home soon.

I will be eligible for separation allowance, and plus, we get £1 a day for being here. If we leave the ship and land on the Falklands, we also get hard-line pay which is about an extra 75p a day. Separation allowance is £1.40 a day, less tax.

The crew are very nice and helpful. So far, a few lads have been seasick. Anyway darling, don't worry about me, I'll try and look after myself. Please look after yourself and keep your chin up. I love and miss you very much. All my love to you and the children. Good night and God bless you. I will write again soon.

Your ever loving Pomme. xxxx

These letters from Pierre clearly indicate his upbeat mood and emotions. Here is another one dated 18th May 1982-Freetown Africa.

My darling Pomme,

Well here we are darling. We have arrived this morning in Freetown. The weather is really hot and muggy, but bearable under the circumstances.

I am fine and hope you are too. I love and miss you very much. We are being drilled and getting fitter with PT every day including Sunday.

Today I performed an operation on board the ship, on a bloke who had to have a big abscess on his bum cut out. When we leave here tomorrow, we will head for the Ascension Islands where he will get off, lucky sod.

I hope to post you some mail when we get there, as we can't post any at the moment.

We may have to stop there for a couple of days, and then proceed, nobody knows yet, as they won't tell us for security reasons.

I have been taking a few pictures and hope to post you the films when I can, okay. Are you looking after yourself, I hope so. Don't forget to check your bike and take care. Send my love to the children.

The ship is being blacked out, so no lights are visible, and sometimes we are confined to our cabins, yuk!

This port is very small, a bit like Penang.

So to pass the time, some of my boys and roommates, are growing a moustache for fun, and the one with the funniest at the end of a set period of time, will get a trophy. Ha. Ha.

Anyway darling I am not spending much, so I am alright for money. I miss you very much, take care of yourself for me. Good night and God bless you.

xxx Pomme xxx.

As the journey to the South Atlantic continues you can sense the seriousness and anxiety building rapidly. Here is another letter from Pierre to Nina, dated 26th May 1982. Again, these are his words. I don't know who chose the devil's postcode number.

My darling Pomme
16 Field Ambulance RAMC
BFPO 666
26th May 1982

We have now been on active service since last week and are now heading for South Georgia, where we are supposed to transfer ships from the QE2. We don't know which ship we will be on, so just address any letters as above.

The situation is very dangerous at the moment, and we are armed with weapons. Maybe by the time you get this letter, we will have landed already on the Falkland Islands, as this is very slow getting through.

The weather is getting bitterly cold and treacherous and a lot of the lads are seasick. At the moment I am fine, and I hope you are too my darling.

Yesterday we had our last pay parade for goodness knows how long, and everyone was issued £30 whether you wanted it or not. After today we will not do any more PT as it's too dangerous and we are under ship blackout orders.

The sun rises here at 08.30am. The lifeboat drills have intensified and helicopter drills too. Tomorrow we should be in South Georgia and transfer ship, ready for the assault on the Falklands.

This brigade is 5 Brigade and has the Welsh Guards, Gurkhas, Scots Guards and Commandos and Marines, plus all the others that support, like us the medics.

Information is hard to get. So we don't know if we will have to land at Port Stanley or Goose Green or Darwin, so it's anybody's guess.

I only hope this is over soon, so I can get back home to you and the children. I love you all and miss you dearly my darling. Please write soon, as I only received Juliette's letter so far and I long to hear from you. I don't know when or how I will be able to write again, but I will try my best.

Give my love to everyone at home and look after yourself for me and let me know what is happening at home.

Remember don't put the ships name on the address, okay!
Bye for now darling, God bless you all, your loving husband

xxx Pomme xxx.

They were then told that they could not risk taking the QE2 to the Falklands and that they would have to tranship to the ship *Norland*, which was standing off. That meant moving all the FST's kit onto a smaller vessel through a door in the QE2s side. It had to be manhandled and then lowered by nets onto the deck and then several journeys made out to the *Norland*. The fighting arms took priority over them, quite naturally, but all this took less than 24 hours. All the time they were there, they were a sitting target for enemy aircraft.

The *Norland* sailed around midnight for Ajax Bay, a few days away. As she turned into wind, the weather deteriorated. It was the worst storm for a long while. The ship was plunging into the waves, corkscrewing and taking on water. It was almost impossible to sleep, as all the bedding was sodden with sea water, and worse.

The storm ran out of steam as they approached the Falklands. They knew they would soon be entering Ajax Bay, where the Parachute Field Ambulance and the Marines Field Surgical Teams were already deployed, also known as the Red and Green Machine FST.

First light came and Pierre got his first glimpse of the Falklands. Brown, barren, steel-grey seas, windy, no trees, just like the Scottish moorland, and certainly no boozers. It was raining, sleeting and downright miserable.

They had formed one big long snake-like queue all around the ship, waiting to board their landing craft. They seemed to be there for hours, moving only inches at a time. At last it was their turn. They were ordered to march to the other side of Ajax bay and camp at, or near, the settlement. The reality was that there was nothing there, just rock and peat bog, stones and more stones.

The Sir Galahad is ostensibly a roll-on, roll-off ferry, shallow draught and not too stable in heavy seas, just like the cross-channel ferries. As it has an open car deck and the ability to open its bow doors, it is not a very safe prospect and would sink rapidly as it has no watertight compartments which could be shut off. Pierre and the whole of 55 Field Surgical Team, plus elements of 5 Brigade Troops, were on board for the last leg of the sea voyage.

The trip back to Fitzroy was quiet, the sea calm and the wind had died down. Leaving late means arriving late, so it was mid-morning before they got into Fitzroy Sound, went to the mess deck in batches for breakfast, went to bunk deck, then went to the car deck to see what is happening. They were not allowed on deck or on the bridge, and there was nothing from the tannoy. The troops nicknamed this area "Bomb Alley", because of the lack of cover and their vulnerability position to air attack.

The float leaves and the bow doors were closed. That was the last time they saw those doors open, as when they closed they jammed and were never reopened. That meant the main deck above the car deck had to be opened, which took forever.

Once accomplished, the roof over the guardsmen's heads was effectively removed and they were exposed to the elements.

It would have been quicker and relatively easy to disembark through the bow doors. Now nets had to be lowered into the hold, boxes of ammo had to be manhandled instead of the use of pallets into the nets, hauled up then lowered to the floats, then again manhandled onto the floats. Very time-consuming and very tiring for the men.

One of Pierre's letters to Nina from the Falklands:

28th May 1982

My darling Pomme

How are you and the children?

I hope you are all well. As for me I'm fine so far. Yesterday we transferred from the QE2 to a North Sea Ferry ship, the "Norland". We left Gritviken, South Georgia, in the early hours of the morning and are now well on the way to the Falklands.

We rendezvous sometime tonight with other ships and our possible destination is the San Carlos bay on the west side of East Falklands, now known as "Bomb Alley". We are close behind the Paras, who took Darwin and Goose Green, but who have sustained casualties.

This ship darling is full of cannon holes and has been attacked time and again, I pray to God that I come out of this alive and well. Pray for me.

I want you to know that should I not come back, I love you very dearly and our children. Please look after them and yourself, as I wouldn't like you to be unhappy. Just remember I have always loved you and always will.

The weather is very bad and we are going through a storm. It's also very cold and lots of icebergs in the sea around us. The crew and men of this civilian ship have already shot down a Skyhawk aircraft.

We are low on rations and water is already rationed. We are not allowed to shower or wash so needless to say we all stink.

We have seven Argentinian prisoners on board, the youngest is only 15 years old. The Paras have taken 900 prisoners. Yesterday, in the fighting their C.O. was killed. Our suitcases have been taken from us and they may get sent back home or to Ascension. Nobody knows.

Seasickness is a problem on board, but so far I'm fine.

Our kit is very heavy to carry and therefore we have had a few casualties with smashed legs and arms as it's difficult to stand or move on board. Please write to me my darling as I haven't heard from anyone yet except Juliette. God bless you all, I miss you dearly and I love and can't wait to get back home to you all. All my love always.

Your ever loving husband
xxx Pomme xxx

I must thank Colonel Jim Ryan for the following excerpts from his diary:

A personal reflection on the Falkland Islands War of 1982 by JM Ryan, OBE OStJ, FRCS, MCh, DMCC, Hon FCEM, Col L/RAMC(V) Emeritus Professor of Conflict Recovery, UCL, UK & International Professor of Surgery, USUHS, Bethesda, MD, USA.

On April 2nd 1982 Argentine troops invaded the Falkland Islands by sea and air. By April 5th the first ships of the British task force had put out to sea. Civilian liners and ferries were requisitioned as troop ships, and a 200-mile exclusion zone was declared on April 12th. In seven weeks a task force of 28,000 men and over 100 ships was assembled and sailed 8,000 miles. The invasion to retake the islands took place on the 21st May - war was joined. Ten thousand men were landed on a barren shore and within three and a half weeks the Islands were retaken and the war was over.

The war would create novel problems for the Defence Medical Services. Lines of communication and resupply lines were over 8,000 miles. The war would take place in winter with virtually no usable buildings or other infrastructure in which to locate medical assets, including field surgical teams.

In 1982 Colonel Jim Ryan (then a Major) was a 37-year-old Senior Specialist in Surgery in the sixth and final year of higher professional training programme and seconded to St Peters Hospital in Chertsey. It is worth pausing for a moment to reflect on this old and discarded training programme.

Three years of general professional training, followed by six years of higher training, had resulted in exposure to the generality of surgery. It included postings to nine separate hospitals, including three NHS secondments to St Bartholomew's, Hackney and St Peters Hospitals with training in general, orthopaedic, plastic, neurosurgical, thoracic and vascular surgery - an unimaginable variety today.

All military surgeons in training at that time had very similar training programmes. The aim was to produce a surgeon trained in the generality of surgery and ready to work alone or in small groups in field surgical facilities. This system of training probably gave the surgeons who would deploy a training edge not available to civilian trainees of the period.

This was also the age before war surgery workshops, Definitive Surgical Trauma Skills (DSTS) courses and the myriad of other training opportunities, including overseas secondments, available to today's military surgeons and their teams.

Training in the art and science of war surgery prior to 1982 was not easy. Military surgeons "cut their teeth" during secondments to the military wing Musgrave Park hospital in Northern Ireland. The troubles were in full swing and a generation of surgical consultants such as Bill McGregor, Bill Thompson and Brian Mayes had learnt their trade during post-colonial conflicts in far-flung places like Cyprus, Aden, Malaya and Borneo.

There was, in short, an institutional memory for the surgery of war which would become evident as the Falkland Islands war progressed.

The military surgeon's bible and almanac at that time was the latest edition of the *Field Surgery Pocket Book,* edited by Kirby and Blackburn, which became essential reading for all deployed military surgeons, irrespective of previous experience or colour of cloth.

It is also worth giving an overview of the medical support for the task force, which included the Fleet at sea and the ground invasion force. The Medical Branch of the Royal Navy was doubly tasked and had the greatest impact on medical operations. They had to provide medical support for the Fleet, with the additional responsibility of providing comprehensive care ashore for the Marines of 3 Commando Brigade, two Battalions of the Parachute Regiment and the Brigade support elements, which included special forces and air assets.

At sea the Royal Navy Medical Branch provided for what would now be described as 1st Role and enhanced 2nd Role assets throughout the Fleet. They also had the additional tasking of manning the only hospital ship, SS Uganda, and its support ambulance ships, which provided medical evacuation by sea.

On land each Commando Battalion was provided with two Commando Medical Officers RN and supporting medical elements.

The Marine Commando Medical Squadron was deployed on the beach-head at Ajax bay with two Royal Navy Surgical Support Teams (SSTs) and their supporting elements acting as an Advanced Surgical Centre (ASC).

The Royal Army Medical Corps provided Regimental Medical Officers (Army) to each major field unit (2 to the Parachute Battalions) and manning for Regimental Aid Posts (RAPs). Surgical support was also provided.

Initially this consisted of two FSTs from the Parachute Clearing Troop of 16 Field Ambulance RAMC to reinforce the ASC. Later 16 Field Ambulance deployed to provide definitive 2nd role medical support for the forces ashore.

Mobilisation to the South Atlantic was fast, furious and frenetic, however it was characterised by what many medics would still recognise - an off the truck, on the truck mentality, shrouded in a fog of uncertainty. Colonel Jim Ryan was assigned to table two of 55 FST, mobilised in Aldershot.

55 Field Surgical Team was the operational reference under which all the Royal Army Medical Corps medical support for the Falklands War was organised. It consisted of two separate surgical teams.

The first named anaesthetist was one Major H Hannah. That is, until it was realised that this was Helen Hannah, a woman. Not just any woman, but the widely admired and redoubtable Major Helen Hannah RAMC. This caused consternation. The British Armed Forces were not ready for a woman on their battlefields and she was quickly replaced by the equally well-known Lt Col Jim Anderson RAMC, who would be appointed OC 55 FST with two surgical teams. FST One was commanded by Major David Jackson (Sgt Pierre Naya's team) and the second team, commanded by Jim Ryan.

Sadly, Colonel Helen Hannah passed away after a brief illness in May 2013. An anaesthetist who was much respected by all OTTs, she will be missed by all who knew and worked with her.

Colonel Jim Ryan's diary reveals that 55 FST departed Aldershot on the 12th May 1982 at 0430 under the command of Jim Anderson and two hours later embarked on the QE2 in Southampton. Work was still under way on the helipad and elsewhere.

At their first "O" group assembly they were told without a trace of humour that the ship had been re-designated LPLL - Landing Platform-Luxury Liner. Keeping a straight face was difficult, but it was a serious matter.

She put to sea at 1600 hours with no one believing that the team would get much past the English Channel. All were hoping for a last-ditch political solution to the escalating scenario of war.

Colonel Jim Ryan kept a diary throughout the campaign and it helps to illustrate the surreal atmosphere on board. It seemed bizarre to go to war on the world's finest luxury liner. A few diary entries reflect the mood on board:

12th May: retired to the 1st class bar for large gins at 2100hrs-retired to bed at 2330 hrs!

13th May - Lifeboat drill ad nauseam.

15th May - superb lunches - fresh salmon yesterday, fresh crab today and wonderful wines.

15th May - My first operation at sea, an appendicectomy on a young combat engineer in the QE 2 operating theatre.

17th May - Captain's cocktail party!! It became increasingly easy to imagine that we were on a holiday cruise, at least for the officers.

Reality checked in when active service conditions were declared. The QE2, initially bound for the Falkland Islands, now turned away and headed for South Georgia. Why?

The given explanation was a threat from submarines. This would lead later to a spectacular slur by the crew of the P&O vessel SS *Canberra*, which went directly to the Falkland Islands to offload her troops. Sometime later her crew hung a sheet over the side with the ditty 'P&O cruises where Cunard refuses'. But it must be said that all who cruised on the QE 2 retain an enormous affection for her.

As one who never left the safety of the Advance Surgical Centre (ASC), apart from the ill-fated sea journey on the *Sir Galahad*, Colonel Jim Ryan confines his remarks to the surgical support for the wounded at the ASC at Ajax Bay. A time traveller from the Boer War or the First World War would have recognised the ASC at Ajax Bay.

It was situated in a meat refrigeration factory facing the San Carlos Water near San Carlos settlement. It was ideal in many respects, vast and open and lending itself to compartmentalisation into operating theatres, wards primitive laboratory and living accommodation for staff and supplies.

A nearby area of open ground facilitated landing by helicopters delivering wounded from the battlefields. On the down side, the ASC was filthy and dusty, rendering effort at cleanliness nigh impossible.

There were no windows and no air conditioning. The building was heated by air pumps delivering hot air.

A personal reflection from Jim Ryan must include the bombing of the RFA logistic ships RFA *Sir Tristram* and *Sir Galahad*, which took place on the morning of 8th June 1982. *Sir Galahad*, carrying Welsh Guards rifle companies and elements of 16 Field Ambulance including the two teams of 55 FST (Pierre was in team 1), arrived off Fitzroy settlement. The ship should have anchored in Bluff Cove, some five miles away, but could not get up the narrow channel to the planned disembarkation beach.

For reasons beyond this review, disembarkation at Fitzroy was delayed. Some elements of 16 Field Ambulance, including Number One team, had got ashore, but the remaining troops including Jim Ryan's team, stayed aboard. It seems surreal now with the passage of years.

With the departure of 16 Field Ambulance and Major David Jackson, Jim Ryan and a group of other officers retired to the wardroom. Lunch was taken and the group stayed in the wardroom comforted by tots of whisky, hot coffee and a dubious movie on the wardroom TV monitor.

The bombing of the *Sir Galahad*

Colonel Jim Ryan continues to say that some time later and without warning, Sir Galahad and Sir Tristram were bombed by a flight of Argentinian fighter bombers. Chaos ensued.

Those of us in the ward room were thrown from our seats by the explosions, we were shaken but uninjured and were now trapped in a blacked out and smoke filled room.

Shortly after recognising our situation we were quickly rescued by a young unnamed 2nd Lieutenant in the Welsh Guards, who found a hatch behind the bar which led out to a passageway going forward and out onto the open deck. The scene there looked chaotic but we quickly realised that a very large number of our comrades had been killed and a greater number wounded, most of them on the tank deck which had taken a direct hit. Others taking the air out in the open were also killed.

Among the dead was Major Roger Nutbeem, second in command of 16 Field Ambulance. Lt Col Jim Anderson, officer commanding 55

FST and anaesthetist with number two team, had also been outside and was badly injured.

All the FST equipment, along with much of 16 Field Ambulance stores was destroyed. The ship was abandoned and many, including Colonel Jim Ryan, clambered into dinghies and life boats. Others were winched directly off the ship by helicopters hovering over the deck. These pilots and crews displayed extreme gallantry.

The ship was on fire and exploding ammunition was propelled skywards towards the rescuing helicopters. The survivors came ashore at Fitzroy and were cared for by those already ashore.

Colonel Ryan remembers being sheltered by WO2 Les Viner MBE RAMC OTT , who was under a mound of peat, smoking his cigarette and drinking whisky from his water bottle. For a time at least, Jim Ryan, while safe and well, was incapable of providing direct assistance to the ongoing rescue effort.

News of loved ones and events in the Falklands War was extremely patchy, and events were not known for several days after.

I must thank Max Arthur OBE, the military historian and author, for allowing me to use the interview he did with Pierre. Pierre often spoke of his fondness and rapport he had for Max, who for over two years interviewed servicemen who took part in the Falklands War for his book published in 1985 called "Above All, Courage". He received first-hand accounts, including Pierre's description in his own words, of events of that fateful day 8th June 1982. This is Pierre's narrative of events.

The first inkling I had of us being attacked was this loud roaring, whooshing noise and I looked up just in time to see an aircraft zooming past, it was flying so low you could tell it was going to rocket or shell us. I instantly registered the colour was wrong. It was a dingy, brownie, chocolate colour. I shouted "It's not ours" and simultaneously someone else shouted "Hit the deck, hit the deck!" then bang, it struck a direct hit and all hell broke loose!

This massive orange fireball started the devastation. It burnt blokes, it killed blokes. Everywhere there was the screaming of men in agony, pain, shock, fear, panic. It all happened in seconds. I was very bewildered and struggling around totally dazed. It was pitch black and I could feel this intense heat burning the back of my head, then I realized my backpack was on fire and burning the back of my head, so I pulled it off and beat out the flames. Everywhere around me was in chaos. My first thought was that we'd been wiped out. I couldn't see a thing, all I could smell was the burning flesh and metal and this acrid smoke. It was stifling and the heat was scorching my lungs. All I wanted to do was get out from the tank deck. People were screaming and shouting in pain. All I wanted to do was to get the hell out of there.

I knew there was a hatch behind me so I made a beeline for that. Needless to say, there must have been about 100 other people with the same idea, some of whom were in a terrible mess. I managed to haul myself and pull others up two flights of stairs towards daylight. On the way up I grabbed this injured guardsman by the belt and tried to get him on the top of the deck rung by rung. He was screaming in agony and pain and kept on saying "mind my leg, mind my leg", but of course he had lost his leg, it was a phantom pain. He was too heavy for me to carry and we both fell backwards down the stairs, but I struggled and somehow managed to get him up the stairs and on the deck. How I got him out of there I don't know, it must have been pure adrenaline at work. I'd got my arm round this poor sod and took him to the bow of the ship to evade the smoke. All the time I was carrying him his bone was hitting the deck and leaving a trail of blood as his shattered stump was being dragged across the deck.

It was chaos everywhere on deck. Smoke and flames were billowing up from below where the bomb had hit, through the opened hatches of the ship. Ammunition was exploding and there were blokes running around screaming because their plastic all weather gear had caught fire and was sticking to them, burning their skin away, it was pitiful to watch them trying to tear it off in panic, pain, screaming, and rolling around on deck as their gear stuck to their skins, frying them alive. The areas of the body exposed most at the moment of flash were mostly face, neck, ears, hair and hands. Some were completely burnt from the neck, skins black and swollen. I'd never seen anything like it. That was an awful sight, such pain, such terrible pain as they were just rolling about on the decks.

This was the fastest my mind had ever worked. I was trying to decipher what was going on and sort out priorities. I wanted to find the others, my mates, but I couldn't. It felt as if I had been caught up in a big machine that was going round and round. Helicopters were suddenly appearing through the dense black smoke and men were jumping off the ship onto lifeboats, into the flaming seas and some being winched off by the helicopters. People were shouting orders and instructions and all the time there were explosions after explosions and flames everywhere.

I didn't have time to think. If they'd attacked us again I wouldn't have known it because there was so much smoke and confusion, it was horrendous, with loud bangs of ammunition exploding. I couldn't see any doctors or other medics working. I found out later they'd been taken off before the bomb struck. I thought I was the last medic alive. So I thought, "Come on, Pierre, you're the only medic alive, get to it". So I got stuck in with what medical kit I had, a pair of military scissors, which could cut even through bone. The rest had been blown to pieces, wiped out.

So I got on my knees and started to cut away at some of the badly burnt clothes to expose the wounds and help alleviate pain. I became a focus for people as they knew at least someone was there to help.

The NCOs were marvellous, keeping everyone calm, beginning to get a grip on the situation, calming the distressed and organizing lines of injured men for me to see and talking to them while they waited.

I began smashing up crates of wood to make splints, because there was nothing else. The Welsh Guards who'd survived came by and dropped their personal field dressing for me to use, others would give me their intravenous drips or held someone down while I got at his injuries. Everyone rallied round as they got over the initial shock and were doing all they could to help me. I didn't have time to look up, I couldn't answer anyone, I'd just say to one of them, "You grab that, just hold it there and I'll start putting up an intravenous drip". I would start infusing the injured. I managed to get a few drips into the very worst injured, those who had legs and ankles blown off.

I have never seen such horrific injuries as these, and have never seen action in all my twenty years of service in the Army. I don't know how I kept a sober head on me at the time. All I remember is treating guys, trying to put a figure of eight bandage round some poor bugger's legs which was smashed up, then kicking a wooden pallet to pieces trying to make splints from it, it was all very primitive. I was putting the field dressing over this fellow's stumps, I then grabbed someone's webbing straps to use as a tourniquet on what was left of his leg, and using a guy's bayonet to tighten it, stopping the river of blood, looking up at the poor devils face to see his face was swollen to twice its size like a pumpkin and was completely black with flash burns.

All the time senior RAMC Warrant Officer Mick McHale, the other medic and RSM, was organizing everything in the background. I was so glad he was alive and had survived the bomb. He was getting the casualties off the ship, he'd come alongside and say "Which one, Pierre, which one next?", as I would point them out in order of priority. Then I'd go back on to the next poor sod. It was decisions, decisions, could I leave him, should I go on to save one who was dying? How much time have I got? Will this bloody ship blow up? Who's next for the chopper? All this was just rushing through my mind. I just carried on, totally absorbed ,working at a frantic pace for what seemed an eternity, doing what I was trained for and helping others.

Over everything hung the fear of another attack from the air or the ship blowing up under me.

A three-ringer Naval officer came up and said, "Can I help?" so I said, "Yes, sir, that one there, shunt him off quick". The lad had lost a leg and had the other broken, as well as one of his arms. I stuck in an intravenous drip in him, but of course we couldn't strap him in a harness as there was this stump. So this naval officer suggested we use a pallet. We laid the lad out and tried to hook the harness round with rope, but as the chopper pulled it up he rolled off in agony. So we called for the harness again and somehow this time wrapped it round him and got him up there. He was the last of the severe casualties, so then I started on the burns victims.

On this blazing hulk of Sir Galahad I had been working flat out, all I could do was start cutting the plastic clothing as it had impregnated their skin and was still smouldering.

Where the lads had grabbed hold of red hot hand railings they had 'de-gloved' the palms of their hands, and their skin had fused to bunch up all the fingers, so I had to cut down between the webs to separate the fingers, all this without anaesthetic drugs or pain killing injections.

Some of the lads were still burning because they couldn't use their hands. There was no water on the ship. If I could pee on them to cool their burning hands I would. All that bloody sea and we didn't have any water. It was the exposed areas of the body which really suffered, the face, the neck, the ears, the hair, the hands, whatever was exposed at the time of the flash got scorched. Many of those lads will carry their scars all their lives. Some were completely burnt from the neck up, no hair, no eyebrows, all black and swollen. I wouldn't recognize them now. While I was waiting to get the last of the burns cases off, I could see one particular lad in pain. There wasn't a thing I could do for him except loosen his collar where the plastic had burnt into his neck. He was holding his fingers apart where I had just cut them to free his fused fingers, and he was standing there bewildered and exhausted, awaiting evacuation. I had a packet of cigarettes, so I lit one and put it in his mouth as he couldn't hold on to it. The pleasure of his grin was wonderful, said it all, as he stood there holding his blackened and bleeding hands in the air puffing away merrily. Later I met blokes who, the moment they hit the beach, started smoking for the first time in their lives. It was the heat of the moment. The adrenaline was flowing something shocking. It was like being very high, but it wasn't a good high, it was a fearful thing. I'd never seen such horror in all my life. Slowly we got them all off.

The chopper pilots performed miracles with dangerous manoeuvres time and time again flying over the blazing and smoke emitting ship very closely, trying to blow the dinghies and lifeboats away from the still-exploding ship with the downdraught from the rotor blades. They saved over three hundred lives that day.

I realized I had been on my knees for probably over an hour, tending the wounded on the now red hot melting deck, so my knees were in not too good a condition. But we'd done it, we'd got everyone off.

Then I thought, "Okay, you can get off now". It was time to get away. Everyone else had gone and so had all the lifeboats. Then for the first time I looked over the side of the ship to see where we were, I never done this, we had been down in the tank deck when it happened, so I never did see the land. Now I could see it, it would be a very long swim, and that's if I survived the high jump into the icy freezing waters below. I'd survived the bombing and fire and now I was going to drown and die.

I stood on the side of that ship on this beautifully clear day. I knew I wouldn't last longer than five minutes in the water, but if I stayed on board I was going to die anyway with the explosions of ammunitions, bullets and rockets going off in all a directions. I knew I'd had it. I had lost my helmet during the initial explosion and thought that any minute now I'd get it in the head. I thought, "I can't just stand here. I've got to get off." so I started to take my boots off, and prepare to take my chance, albeit a very slim one, in the water.

Suddenly a Naval officer came out of the smoke and shouted, "A chopper's coming." This man I believe today to have been the captain of Sir Galahad, Captain Phil Roberts. I was the last man off the burning ship besides the captain.

I have never been more grateful to see a pilot in my life, and, as I was winched on board, I put the sign of the cross on his visor. He just smiled. He was so young. They saved our lives that day, they saved over 300 lives.

As we veered away from the ship I began to tremble and shake like a leaf. I'd survived, got my legs, hands and was in one piece. Out of our advanced party we had lost our major, a lance corporal, and a private. When I got ashore the first voice I could just about make out was our Regimental Sergeant Major (RSM). He was shouting at me but I hadn't realized that I had gone deaf out there on the ship, with the constant excruciating explosions which took place. I was so pleased to see him and the rest of my mates that I gave them a hug and a kiss.

As we were taken to some huts I saw all the doctors busy and working and was delighted as I thought they were all killed. I immediately started helping to tend the wounded, putting up drips and getting the injured lads ready for casevacing. I also saw the commanding officer and said, "I'm sorry, Sir, I've lost my pistol on the Galahad. There is my magazine". I felt really guilty that I had lost it among the chaos. Later the RSM gathered all 16 Field Ambulance and some other medics and did a head count to see who was alive, who was dead, who was missing and who had been casevac'd, and it was then that I realized I was really stone deaf. This officer came up and he was saying something like, "Thank you for the good job you did on the ship for the men". I can lip read a little bit, because some of my wife's relatives are a little hard of hearing, and I'm used to talking to some of their friends who are deaf. The next thing I knew, the RSM had detailed two lads to look after me, "just in case we have an air raid", as I was still in shock. The RSM through the estate manager at Fitzroy, had discovered an empty house which they allowed us survivors to use. When we got there every body there said, "Keep the house clean. Don't smoke, and if you do use the ashtrays. Take your boots off, don't put them on the floor. When you leave clean up behind you etc". It was like coming from hell to suburbia! So we all huddled on the floor on the carpet and just slide down and slept there, almost upright, half crouching, half sitting. I had my head under the sideboard for a bit of protection in case somebody came over at night.

It was a pitiful sleep because all my thoughts were racing, refusing the sleep I desperately needed. What had happened? What had gone wrong? Did I do enough? How were my mates? Because even then there were some of my friends I hadn't seen. I didn't see my Warrant Officer, Les Viner, for ages after I got on to the shore. With all this turmoil that had been going on, the feeling was incredible. First of all of being alive, and second how fortunate that I was, and third, what a blooming disaster it had been. It was hard getting the sense of death out my system.

Of course I thought of my wife Nina, and my four daughters back home. I thought of how I could contact her, because this news was bound to break some way. It had to get back some time and she'd hear it through the grapevine. I had nothing to write on, no paper, so eventually when I did write a letter it got to her about three weeks after the incident!

It was only when I got to Stanley, when things were quieter, that I could sneak *off to the Cable and Wireless place and send her a telegram. Just a few words. "I'm safe and well, Love Pierre." It cost me every penny I had, but it was worth it.*

I was woken up by someone saying, "You're going back. A helicopter's coming to take you away. Leave your boots for the lads who are left behind as survivors, they got no boots." So I took off my boots and left them. They took us to this helicopter in just what we stood up in, and the next thing I know is that I am once more back on a ship, I presume near Ajax Bay, which we had sailed out of thirty-six hours ago. It was dark, as it was night time, and darkened ship routine was in force. It was almost as though it did not happen, you're gone and thirty-six hours later you were back. But you were back as a different person.

My mind was totally frazzled and, of course while we were on there we had a Red Alert and were bundled below decks into a bunk area once again. Of course the hatch was closed down again on top of us, and I thought, "Oh my God, not again". But nothing happened. What mental torture.

Then I went to see the ship's doctor, who told me that my hearing would come back and it was nature's way of shutting down without damaging the ears. He then asked if I wanted to do something, so he sent me to work in the sick bay to help with the three badly burnt casualties from Galahad. I think one of them was the cook, his face was twice its normal size. I ended up trying to look after these three lads in order to give the ship's medic a break. It took my mind of things until we were lifted back to Ajax Bay, where at least we were able to relax for a day. The Paras and Marines knew what had happened and they looked after us, making hot meals. After re-supply we were then flown by chopper to Fitzroy again, meeting up with mates.

Some of us were accommodated in a house occupied by a very kind family who already had an assortment of troops lodging there. I remember one evening the lady of the house produced some rice pudding and, from somewhere, bottles of whisky appeared.

Then, what a joy, she gave us a guitar which I enjoy playing. Of course, I soon started playing and we had a sing-song. I ended up being spoon-fed rice pudding by an artillery major, who kept on saying "Play it again, Sam". He really got drunk that night. He was trying to get death out of his system as well, which I totally understood.

We all had a job to do and I would have felt guilty if I hadn't done it. I could certainly have gone off the Galahad straight away, but I didn't, it never crossed my mind. I don't know, perhaps it was my upbringing, my background, my family life, but to me all those men were my family. They were all my mates, my comrades, they were looking to me as a Medic. I just did it without thinking about it. Those lads were hurting, hurting very bad. I just had to do something.

I felt great afterwards, I felt I had achieved something, contributed some small part in all this horrific mess. I felt satisfied, felt proud, but also sad.

Later I stood for hours on the cliff above Bluff Cove and looked and stared at the Galahad. The tears were just rolling down my face. I couldn't believe that this was the ship that had brought us so far, and there it was, burning in the water. It was an eerie red glow in the dusk. I stood on the shoreline just mesmerised looking at her. It was pitiful. She burnt for days, as we expected her to go up in one big explosion, break in half and sink, but somehow, for some reason she never did. The entire bridge had caved in and the topside was black and charred, except in patches where the paint had peeled off and the metal shining in the last rays of sun and I was overwhelmed with sadness. There were just the occasional bang, and a bout of smoke, then it would go all quiet again.

The tugboat "Typhoon" towed the burning wreckage out to sea and sank her. This poem and tribute were written by Jack Crummic, the bosun of the tug.

The Eve of the Sinking of the Sir Galahad

Sir Galahad, Sir Galahad
My heart for you doth weep
You're going to die tomorrow
So that fifty souls can sleep

For on a cold June morning
Rained madness from the sky
Our soldiers screamed and perished
You heard and knew not why.
You burnt and writhed and twisted
And you knew all their pain
But you kept it all within you
Your memories and our slain.
Your burning funeral pyre
Was there for all to see
A reminder of man's inhumanity
And of how stupid we can be.
But when you die, Sir Galahad
The picture God will see
Mankind washing its conscience
In this cold and bitter sea.
So Sir Galahad, we will sink you
We will send you to the deep
Lie quiet in your watery grave
And guard our soldiers sleep.
For your name will stand in history
As guardian of our slain
You will die with honour
While men will bear the shame.

I have overriding impressions about the war. First is the pain, there was a lot of pain. Everywhere you went there was pain, because that's what I came into contact with. Not so much fear, but pain. Pain and death. The ones who were coming back to us were the ones who were alive. The dead weren't coming back to us, and that is another kind of pain.

The second thing that really hit me was the desolation of the Falklands. There was nothing there. It was a godforsaken place, empty ,cold, bleak, naked, and without a single tree. It was almost as if there was no life. You wondered what you were doing there. As for the thousands of sheep, I didn't see any, apart from two or three running on a hillside. The people kept within their houses, you saw two or three locals, that's all. There really was nothing there, it was desolate, cold and bleak, a very inhospitable place.

The final impression would be humility. It has to be. I was awed by what happened. I was absolutely gripped by the throat. The humility of it all, how pitiful a person can be in a situation among such horror, such terror against all those incredibly powerful weapons. You just feel so insignificant.

I went through an experience which I'll never, ever forget, which has brought me closer to God, because it was certainly Him that carried me through and kept me alive. I used to say my prayers every night I was out there, even in the trenches and sangars. I used to pray I wouldn't get injured or killed. I didn't want to come home in a bag.

I feel humble, and lucky that I survived. But it still comes back, it plays on your mind, especially at night .You see, the experience was so traumatic that it hurt to talk about it, so I just clammed up. I couldn't talk about it to anyone. A thousand emotions still rage through me when I think of it all. Of course we put on a brave face, we can't collapse in a heap. I hope over the years it will fade.

People ask me, "Why did you get a medal?" But how and where can you start and give them an answer in one sentence? You can't. It was all too real. The one thing I am trying to do is shed the Galahad, but often it catches me when I'm unaware, and images flash back. So I bottle it up.

I'm not alone, many of us have done that. We can't really tell our wives what we went through. There are certain things I will never tell. There are also experiences I shared that, unless you were there, with my comrades, would seem sentimental and incomprehensible to an outsider, like sharing the same plate, the same fork, the same sleeping bag, the last fag, surviving, making a joke out of the misery, lads with black, burnt faces and you'd say "Cor, you look rough, what hole have you come from?" Anything, anything to break the tension and ease the pain.

They were brave men. Sometimes we got the impression from the media that we were losing, and that gripped us. We thought, "if we lose here, we've had it. We must not lose." It gave us more incentive to go on. You just worked, no matter what you were doing, whether you were the cook, or digging a sandbank, you did it with zeal, you got stuck in. I shudder to think what would have happened if we'd lost. I don't know what would have happened, I really don't. We couldn't get off and there was no way they could take all of us off. I can't imagine being marshalled into Buenos Aires as a British prisoner.

When people talk about heroism I think of the Paras and Marines and the others who had to fight the enemy, tooth and nail, eye to eye, it takes real guts to do that, it really does. As far as I am concerned, heroism is a bit like madness.

You had to be mad to face an enemy in hand to hand fighting. You have to completely detach yourself from the situation presented at the time. You have to jump in with both feet but be completely switched off. You know it's a deliberate act, and you know you might get killed. But you do it. Your either very brave or mad, there is no logic.

I certainly don't consider myself a hero. I just did my job.

The image I conjure up of his heroic deeds makes me extremely proud of my brother Pierre. He was very lucky to be alive and the good Lord was on his side on that day.

Why weren't the doors closed up, that's the sixty four thousand dollar question? That meant the main deck above the car deck had to be opened. Once this was accomplished effectively the roof over the guardsmen was removed and they were exposed to the elements.

Imagine that huge cubic meterage of the car deck filled instantly with black acrid smoke, huge flames, men screaming, men dying, men burning to death. God bless their souls. To give you some idea of the temperature, the aluminium construction of the ship's interior melted and the steel distorted so badly you couldn't recognise the structure.

A few days after the bombing, living rough in makeshift dugout holes, wet through, dirty and no food, they were very hungry. All around them and in abundance were geese. Catching them was something else. So Pierre, using his hunting skills learnt in Dar es Salaam as a teenager, rigged a trap attached to a long piece of string. He had done this on numerous occasions with great success, back home. He tried to persuade an upland goose to walk into the trap. Pierre talked to it in Swahili with a French accent, and just as he was about to pull the string to secure their dinner some dozy Para shot it with an Armalite rifle.

Colonel Ryan's diary states on 12th June: "The attack on Port Stanley to force an Argentinian surrender starts at 0200hrs. We will be busy by morning". It would indeed prove to be a busy day. The team operated on sixteen cases, commencing at 1030 hrs and ending at 2200 hrs. Overall he records that three teams carried out in excess of thirty procedures without fatality. The pattern was now set for the next four days; battles for the mountains were fought by night, with casualties arriving by helicopter at the surgical centres at first light.

The consequence for the wounded was very long delays before evacuation. All were hypothermic to a greater or lesser degree on arrival at the surgical centres. Few were bleeding heavily on arrival, but warming and fluid resuscitation produced dramatic and unexpected recurrences of bleeding. Each day was characterised by a lengthy operating list followed by early to bed.

By 16th June the land battles were over and Port Stanley liberated, although it would be a further day before an island-wide surrender was signed.

It was not until 19 June that personnel were briefed. This delay led to expressions of disgust and lowering of morale. The army FST personnel at Ajax were all *Sir Galahad* survivors. They had been had been living and working in the same clothes for nearly two weeks and were now stinking.

To compound matters, the FST was moved from Ajax Bay to a support ship, *Elk*, and told to wait in the hold. Such was the mood of the team by now that a move to Port Stanley after twenty-four hours probably prevented any outbreak of violence as the FST still held their weapons and ammunition.

In these situations there are two priorities among those affected. In the first place it is very satisfying to know that someone is personally trying to improve your situation and the second is when it's going to happen. Even though they were probably beset with almost equally intractable problems, it was very thoughtless behaviour by movements staff to delay a briefing that would have settled the mood, however uninformative it might be in the circumstances. A briefing, even when there are no hard facts, still inspires trust and goodwill.

Most medical personnel were quickly returned to the UK by ship, as indeed were most of the fighting troops. This cleared the way for fresh units arriving daily to disembark and begin garrison duties. Jim Ryan's FST drew the short straw and stayed pending the arrival of 22 Field Hospital.

The Field Surgical Team was the only resource ashore and, after the departure of the Hospital ship Uganda, the only surgical facility for the population and garrison on land and at sea. It was a very busy period, as there had been very little medical support for the local population since the Argentinian invasion. In addition a number of incidents with mines and missiles kept the casualties coming.

As elements of 22 Field Hospital arrived in small packets, so the FST slowly disintegrated. It was quite sad not to have all been stood down as a unit and to have returned to the UK together as one.

It was widely believed that the Ministry of Defence were keeping a tight hold on all information released to the media. That was to be expected for many reasons, including security. That they were not being forthright was obvious on several newsreel reports. News of our soldiers, sailors and airmen at war in the Falklands was extremely patchy and information on actions on which they might be involved was often delayed for many days.

It was rumoured that Warrant Officer Les Viner MBE OTT I/C of the Field Surgical Team had been severely injured, or even killed, when the *Sir Galahad* was bombed, but he wasn't. Such was the sketchiness of news filtering through.

Letters to Nina

Here is a further collection of letters from Pierre to his wife Nina,'Pomme' as he called her. They date from 12th June, four days after the attack on the *Sir Galahad*, to 10th July. It is clear in the first letter, which is placed out of date order because of its contents, that he suspects his letters are being held up along the line and the cool, calculated way he describes and plays down his own injuries and events on and after that fateful day of the bombing, feels uncomfortable.

6th July 1982
My darling Pomme,

I hope you are well and everything is fine at home. Today I received a whole bunch of letters from you and it was lovely. I miss you very much. But first I must tell you that I think somehow our letters from here are being held up somewhere, and it's obvious this must be the case as you are not receiving my mail telling you that I am fine.

Anyway I will try and explain what's happened since the Galahad.

I was on the Galahad, which was taking us to Fitzroy, when we were bombed and attacked. Thank God darling I survived.

Only my hair on the back of my head caught fire and my clothes, which I quickly put out. I am very well and I'm not scarred or burnt darling.

I only got a few bruises when it happened, but now they are all gone, and my hair is back to normal.

I wrote many letters since and I hope by now you will have received them. At least I tried to explain where I was and what I was doing.

Right now I'm sitting on my bed in my room in Port Stanley hospital, because after the Galahad, we were survivors and sent back to Ajax at San Carlos.

We stayed there for a day, then got sent back to Fitzroy, the site of the bombing, again by helicopters. We worked there as FST 55 No 1 until the surrender.

When it was over we stayed a further two weeks, and then they sent us to Port Stanley Hospital.

When we arrived here Col Andersons team 55 FST No 2 had just arrived from Ajax. It was so nice and comfortable, that they wanted to stay here, so they sent us onto the ship "St Edmunds".

After about four days we had to leave, because other troops needed a wash and rest, so we went back to the hospital.

They told us there that we were not wanted, so they sent us out onto the tanker ship "Fort Toronto" which was outside the harbour. We stayed on here until the C.O. of 2 Field Hospital arrived at Stanley and sent a message to say stay there a little longer, as he was trying to get us home.

In the meantime Cleverly Parker and Col Anderson's team were cracking up back at the hospital. So we got another message to say that they were being sent home, and we had to replace them.

So they eventually they got us off the "Toronto" and now we are back in the hospital working, and 55 FST No 2 team have gone home. The bastards rubber dicked us.

We were then informed by the CO of 2 Field Hospital that if anyone could take it, Les Viner and myself could, so brigade HQ said we had to stay, while they sent the rest back.

Our surgeon Major Jackson, Major Banerjee anaesthetist, Cpl Forshaw from Woolwich and the rest of our team have all gone back. So that's why Les and myself are still here. Yesterday though the CO showed me a signal which said Sgt Partridge-Hogbin from 2 Field and 2 other OTTs have been nominated to come out to relieve us. The RAF are trying to arrange seats for them on a Hercules, as it's the only plane that can land here at Port Stanley at the moment.

Failing that, they may have to fly to Ascension Islands and then by sea to here. So that's good news. At least it's something to hope for, which means I may be home soon darling.

Any way as I was saying, at least we now have a chance of coming home as soon as PH gets here. By now SGT JA, one of the 2 Field Hospital lads who got sent back to UK should have arrive, and hopefully, he will come round and explain the situation to you.

Also Major Jackson, our surgeon, will have arrived by now, as he said he would phone all the wives on his team and explain the situation.

Darling don't send me anything, as I have got enough now to see me through. They found our suitcases on the ship "Norland" which hasn't sunk as you all were told. They were handed back to us.

Fortunately I've still got my tweed jacket and my one good trousers, my nice shirts, good brown shoes, as well as my ties and wash bag. I also have my travelling shoe cleaner pouch.

Unfortunately everything else was lost with the ship Galahad, with the rest of my army kit. I'm not too badly off at the moment, as people have been good and giving us spare socks and a combat jacket and some woolly long johns.

The Red Cross and various ships and people like Oxfam have donated us survival parcels with a spare jumper, shaving kit and even dressing gowns. I've also managed to acquire some new St Michael's brand white underwear, all brand new.

I've also managed to get some tax free whisky and brandy from the ships, for when I come back, as it was so cheap to buy.

Outside it's freezing, and we have had deep snow and sleet now for three days. The weather is atrocious with high winds, but at least we are in the warmth inside.

We hear the rest of 2 Field reinforcement will arrive in about 2 days' time, on or about the 9th July.

So hopefully this letter will put you in the picture.

Love to the children and everyone. Sleep well.
All my love xxx Pomme xxx.

12th June 1982
My darling Pomme

Yesterday we started the push to take Stanley. So far its hard going for our boys, but we have reached our objectives. Needless to say we are very busy with casualties. We have to keep working as and when the casualties come in.

At the moment I am sitting on a mattress in a house that belongs to some islander and Les Viner is in the same room as me. These houses are only made of tin and wood, but its shelter. As for me darling I am fine honestly, and I hope you are too, and also the children. I received your letter today and Nicola's and Yvonne's and it has really been the highlight of the day hearing from you as I haven't had a letter for nearly a month. Thank you darling and please keep writing okay? I also received the cheque card that you sent in this letter of yours so I will sign it and keep it okay?

There is nowhere to draw any money or spend it either, but still I have got it any way. We are only allowed to use these aerogrammes as its free, but the trouble is, where we are, they are getting scarcer to find. The noise outside is terrible, the helicopters never stop flying it seems. Today thank God is the about the only day we haven't been bombed. We can still see the ship that was wrecked by bombs that we were on. It is still burning today and half sunk. It is only about 400 yards off shore here in Fitzroy Creek and next to it is the other assault ship that was also wrecked, the Sir Tristram. A lot of us are wearing second hand clothes and items that have been salvaged or partly burnt, and also clothing that has been taken from bodies or Argentinian prisoners. Last night we have taken about 400 more prisoners and they are outside in a pen and guarded. We are displaying the Red Cross now, so we have to treat their casualties as well. Hopefully soon in a couple of days, maybe we will advance on Stanley and get it over with. At the moment it's very cold and snowed last night. Dysentery is a problem everywhere. Food is scarce and all essential items shared by all the boys especially cigs, tooth paste, boot polish and water.

I pray to God that I will be home soon. Darling keep yourself safe and well for me, and kiss my children for me. Thank all those who all wrote to me as I can't write back okay? Keep a beer in the fridge for me. I love and miss you very much and promise I will take care of myself as best I can. Give my love to all at home and pray for me. Give my love to Mum as well. I will write again when I get the chance. Please write soon, all my love darling.

Yours for always
xxx Pomme xxx

16th June 1982
My darling Pomme

Well dear it's all over, we made it and I'm fine.

I hope you are too. I'm just looking forward to coming home soon. I hear 2 FLD Hospital are coming out, so hopefully they will send us home, maybe in a month's time.

At the moment here it's quiet thank God. We have a lot of prisoners and wounded people to treat and look after. The weather here is cold and sometimes snowy with rain.

Today we walked to the cliffs and looked at our wrecked ship, it's been beached just under the cliffs and it's still burning. Now it's just a question of scrounging anything and everything to survive until they send us home.

Some of the 3 and 5 Brigade lads are already starting to move out. So I hope it's our turn soon. We are just marking time at the moment. They may send us to Stanley before that, as there are a lot of injured people there, and there is a lot of disease also.

As for us we are fine, we just stink. We haven't had a shower or bath since we left home as water is scarce and it's freezing here. We look like tramps honestly, never mind I'll sit in the bath when I get home with a nice toddy eh? A lot of the lads are suffering from trench foot, athlete's foot and just general rot. There is a lot of lice, bed bugs, ticks dysentery and so on.

But so far I am fine. You know me, I'll try and keep warm and have a strip wash now and then. We are just very tired, operating sometimes for sixteen hours nonstop as some of the injuries are horrendous with arms and legs blown off and all sorts.

I hope the girls are alright and everyone at home are fine. Give them my love okay? I miss you all dearly.

Look after yourself darling and I hope I'll be back home soon.

God bless you all. All my love to you darling and keep smiling okay.

I love you.
Your ever loving husband
xxx Pomme xxx

20th June 82
My darling Pomme

Today I received a whole lot of letters from you and the children and Masie and Jacki and Sandy Naya, it was really lovely as I was feeling very low, and it has cheered me up no end. I hope you are alright at home and everything is fine. As for me I'm fine thank God, my bruises are healing and hair is growing nicely .

Today we had a memorial service near the beach here in Fitzroy for all those that died in the two ships that we were on and those who died during the fighting here. Our ship "Sir Galahad" is still burning, as it had a lot of stores and ammunition on it. They are going to try and get on board and salvage a few things if they can and then tow it out into deep water and sink it. It has been declared a

144

war grave. We the FST are fine but we lost Major Nutbeem who was the 2 i/c of 16 Fld Ambulance, he died on the stairway with severe shrapnel wounds of the head and 2 CPLs by the name of Farrell and Preston who also died in the hold. Fitzroy is among small settlement with only about 12 houses and a few barns and at the moment I am lying on the floor of a top room of one of the houses and share this room with six lads, Les Viner, myself, Cliff Forshaw, Ian Macmillan, Rick Gramson and Chris Richards, the chap whose wife you met called Jane. Next door sleeps Major Jackson, surgeon, Major Bannerjee, anaesthetist, and Lt Col Watts, resus officer.

We share everything that we have and help each other. We all stink and need a wash. Everything is rationed. We have no money and haven't been paid for over 3 weeks, and then we could draw only £10. There is a small store here but no one got any money.

Good news, a helicopter has just landed with some beer, hooray!!

We are allowed to buy 4 cans on tick for 75 pence. Great, we have just been told we can get rations cigs on tick as well so that's not bad. We are up to our knees in mud and it's raining and freezing. Today I washed my only pair of skiddies and put them back on before it was dry as it's cold. The blokes are suffering from a bad bout of diarrhoea, vomiting, lice, crabs, scabies and bronchial pneumonia, it's awful! but never mind eh. Maybe in a few months' time when we are relieved we will be home and on the mend. I miss you darling and love you very much. Send my love to all at home and thank them for enquiring about me. Please keep writing okay. I love you dearly.

Bye for now Yours always
xxx Pomme xxx

23rd June 82
My darling Pomme

I hope you are fine and in good spirits. As for me darling I am fine. At the moment I'm on board the ship M.V. St Edmunds in Port Stanley. We arrived here yesterday from Fitzroy. We were sent to the hospital in Stanley to work, and when we got off the helicopter, we bumped into the C.O. and all the advanced party of 2 Field Hospital.

They then told us that as they were there and the rest of 2 Field were on their way, there would be no need to keep the Advance FST which is us at Stanley. So it was tentatively decided that we should be put on board this ship for a couple of days R&R, possibly to stay on it until she sails for home.

We are all praying that they don't change their minds and put us back onshore to carry on working. They may transfer us to another ship here, but we don't know yet.

There is a hell of an argument going on here, whether they need 2 FST'S or 1, if they say 2 then we've had it, we will have to stay. Anyway we have managed to have a shower and shave and are getting some hot meals supplied ,which makes a change.

General Menendez and his senior officers have just been put on board this ship under guard. I don't know why they are here. This is a civvy sea link ship, but is a lot more comfortable than a hole in the mud.

The troops are trying to settle down in Stanley and clean up all the shit that the Argies have shat everywhere, the dirty bastards.

Anyway darling C.P and 3 other OTT'S have volunteered to stay here if they need only one FST, so I pray there is a chance we will be able to get home soon. I met George Bonnelarme and he sends his regards to all. If they don't need the rest of 2 Field who are on their way they may turn them round at the Ascension Islands.

Well darling I miss and love you take care until I get home okay. Send my love to all at home for me and I hope to see you all soon. Congratulations to Fred.

All my love to you and take care and listen to the radio you may hear a message from me.

Love xxx Pomme xxx

26th June 82

My darling Pomme

How are you darling? I hope you are well and in good spirits. As for me I am fine and for a change in reasonably good spirits. Today the powers to be in 2 Field Hospital in Port Stanley Hospital, gave us an order to transfer ship yet again. Up till today we were on the St Edmunds for a few days so-called R&R but all we seemed to do there was work like slaves, cleaning decks, landing cargo and collecting garbage.

Today we transferred ship to the Fort Toronto, which is a big tanker, but at the moment she is carrying mainly water. It only has a small crew and they are fantastic. There are only 23 of us, that is, the entire FST 1, and half a holding section that was bombed on the Galahad. The senior NCOs have been accommodated in the officers' cabins and I am in the chief officer's cabin next to the captain, and it's really luxurious compared to all the other ships we have been on. The food is really first class as we are treated as officers by the civvy crew.

At the moment we are refuelling a ship at sea and it will take four hours and it's dark, we will finish at midnight and then head back for Port Stanley.

The captain, a nice lad, lets me steer the ship whenever I want to relieve the helmsman, Super. I hope you are receiving my letters as I write regularly and I think somewhere my letters are being held up, but never mind its war!

We have no news yet of when we will be coming home but we hope it will be soon, maybe in a month's time or thereabouts. I hope so as they don't need 2 FST teams here. Les Viner and everyone else here is fine and he is on board with me as part of our team and is not injured as you probably heard, he was OK and nothing happened to him at all.

I miss you darling and love you very much and the children too, so take care and keep yourself safe and well for me. Wish mum a happy birthday for me as I think I missed her birthday. She sent me a card for mine, bless her. My writing is shaking as we are going through a minefield now and the ship is vibrating a lot and making the table shake as well. I will write again soon so take care and God bless my love to all at home. I miss you very much. Goodnight ,sleep tight and I hope to see you soon.

I love you my darling.
Yours always xxx Pomme xxx

10th July 82
My darling Pomme

How are you, darling? I hope you are fine and well. As for me, I am just fine and waiting to get home now. Today the "Rangateri" arrived with Pierre Ferrari and all that lot. I haven't seen him yet as the ship is in the outer harbour at the moment and I expect they will come ashore sometime and see us.

Sgt P.H. from 2 Field will be coming out on the 13th July, so that means at the latest he should arrive here on or about the 16th July. We are hoping we will be allowed to catch the next flight out of here, and be home before on or about the 17th to 20th July. Good news eh my darling, I can hardly wait. I am just counting the days now.

Gill Bennett from CMH dropped me a card, which was nice of her, and said she been round to see you. She says you lost weight. Darling you must look after yourself as I worry about you. I hope your tummy is better. Please let me know what is happening, okay? I love you very much my darling and only regret I am not home to give you a hand with things, and keep an eye on you, as I suspect "Sparky" is eating more than you are.

I hope by now Jerry Austin from 2 Field has been round to see you, and also Major Jackson and Col Anderson has phoned you to explain about us out here, and that I'm perfectly alright and well. They promised they would.

Please take care my darling and I am hoping we will be home very soon. Here the weather is very bad with snow and blizzards for the last 3 days now, and it's very cold. There is nothing wrong with Les Viner, and he is fine. Give his mrs my regards okay! Send my love to all at home and the children, as I miss them. Any way darling as soon as I know for sure when we are coming home, I will try and let you know as soon as possible okay?

I love and miss you my light of my life and look forward to my cuddles okay? Sleep well and don't lose any more weight if you can help it okay

God bless and remember I love you, all my love always darling.
xxx Pomme xxx

2nd July 82
My darling Pomme

The person bearing this letter is Jerry Austin, he is from 2 FLD Hospital and was out here in the Falklands with me. Rather than go into a lengthy explanation, I hope he will explain to you what is happening out here.

As for me I am fine and hoping to be home in the near future. Don't get upset darling as to why I didn't come home on the same plane as they did, because as you will gather from what Jerry will have told you, Les and myself have been really "rubber dicked" into staying here a little longer. When I eventually get home, and we have been promised it will be only another fortnight, I will explain all to you okay?

At the moment I am very bitterly disappointed that I'm not home, but I am safe and well and still on the "Fort Toronto" in the harbour, and will be going ashore tomorrow with the rest of them. Myself and Les Viner and a young lad called Macmillan will have to stay at Stanley Hospital and work for another fortnight at least, while we wait for our relief to come out and arrive.

We have been promised by the Commanding Officer it will only be another fortnight, so I hope they are not lying to us, just to keep us quiet. I miss you very much and looking to the day when I am home again.

I received two letters of yours dated 27th June and a card from Mike & Babs for my birthday. I am sorry I can't be home for that but never mind I will cuddle you when I do get there. It's very cold and snowed today. Give everyone my love and the children too. Well darling I hope Jerry explains the situation to you. I love you and take care okay. I am thinking of you all the time and hopefully be home soon. Bye for now darling. I love you very much.

All my love always, yours only
xxx Pomme xxx

No passport for a war hero

While the war and subsequent surrender of the Argentinians was going on, over here in the UK we were all riveted to the frustrating, often erratic news broadcasts by the BBC on television in their daily bulletins on the war's progress.

We wanted to know how Pierre was faring in that winter warfare. The way news was being released made that very difficult to establish, and even with my inside information contacts, it was very difficult to piece together the scattered information so that all the family could feel that Pierre should be all right.

I remember sitting in the Cambridge Military Hospital Aldershot operating theatre coffee room with colleagues watching the news broadcast by the late BBC reporter Brian Hanrahan, on the shores of Bluff Cove, filming and narrating on the still exploding *Sir Galahad*. There were plumes of black smoke from the stricken vessel into which helicopters appeared to be flying, rescue vessels round the ship and approaching the shore full of uniformed men, some shouting instructions, with others, injured and screaming in pain, lying on the pebbled shore and of course troops dying.

I did not know that my beloved brother Pierre was on board doing his heroic deeds when all this was happening, and we all commented on the poor buggers, on board, and what devastation before our very eyes was taking place. That image stayed with me for a long time.

We didn't know of his whereabouts because communications from troops over in the Falklands were either censored and barred by the Ministry of Defence or they did not have any opportunity to do so. I suspect a combination of both took place.

Days later I received a Bluey (a British Forces blue coloured aerogramme letter) from Pierre saying he was well, although injured, and in fact was aboard the *Sir Galahad* when all this carnage was taking place.

That's all he wrote about the conflict. Maybe he was still in shock. That's the sort of person Pierre was. It most certainly showed how strong he was in his mind though, a born survivor reflecting well on his upbringing all those years ago in Dar es Salaam, thanks to our very dedicated and loved parents.

I thought I had lost this one and only bluey he wrote to me from the Falklands all those years past, but after turning the house upside down I finally found it. It is dated 24th June 1982. How could I have lost it?

I now want to share with you exactly what he wrote that day.

Dear Mike and Babs,

I hope my letter finds you in good health and spirits. I'm sorry I could not write before, but I'm sure you'll forgive me, as life for me here has been absolute hell.

I am classified as a survivor of the "Sir Galahad" which got bombed and strafed by the Argies. They hit us on the 8th June and it was bloody horrendous as far as casualties were concerned, I have never seen anything like it. Thank God I survived, as I was in the hold with nearly half the embarked troops waiting to get off. The bombs hit the ammo that we were unloading and all hell broke loose, as it started to explode, killing a lot of blokes. I managed to hit the deck and only my clothes and kit and my hair caught fire. I was very lucky.

We have since been at Fitzroy where we got hit living like tramps in holes of mud and freezing rain and snow. We stink and look terrible, as we are wearing all sorts taken from bodies, casualties and Argie prisoners. We lost everything including the 2 FST's and the ship, which burnt for 3 weeks and has now sunk.

Everything is rationed and there is not much of it anyway. But yesterday we got sent to Stanley by Chinook helicopters and are at present on board a ship called St Edmunds for a couple of days rest and a decent meal and a de-gunj.

The fighting is over except for a few small isolated pockets of Argies. It was dreadful while it lasted as we were bombed and strafed and mortared every day. Thank God it's over and things are getting slowly back to normal, my hair is growing fine. I lost my hearing for a few days by the blast and fireball, but it's almost back to normal now.

Stanley is a mess and so is Fitzroy, Goose Green and Darwin and also Ajax Bay, we have moved around a lot on foot, by chopper and in ships and the Argies really left a mess in more ways than one, the bastards. They booby trap everything that they leave with eventual results.

I must close as I am on duty again on board ship. So take care and all my love to you all at home. I will write again soon when I get more paper. I miss you all terribly and hope to be home in the near future. God bless you all. Have a beer for me on the 4th July as it's my birthday okay? Keep me some wine too! I love you all. Bye for now. your brother Peter. xxxxx

I felt great joy and elation that first he was well, and the possibility of his being commended for his heroic actions was the icing on the cake. Good on you Bruv. I am very proud of him.

His comment on the wine referred to the five gallons of red wine we started on his departure and that I was to save him some to celebrate his homecoming with the family, whenever that might be.

God was looking out for him on that fateful day and I cried with pride and joy, tempered with relief for his survival.

After those events, Pierre had many opportunities to speak openly about his ordeal. Even on his return home he was unable to do so and they remained so strongly etched in his memory that when he tried to recall even some of them he would soon break down in tears.

On family occasions he would only say that he did "things he shouldn't have done as a Catholic." To this day we have never fully understood what he meant by that. We can imagine, but not know. Pierre would start chain smoking and of course all though he liked a drink, his consumption grew.

He was very humble and very sad about the people who lost their lives and the pain they endured, with often tears welling in his eyes. He felt he had received the Military Medal not for himself but for comrades and the Royal Army Medical Corps.

There were many unanswered questions as to why this disaster happened. Why was the landing craft door so damaged that it could not be removed or repaired?

Accounts makes clear that the soldiers should have left the ship hours earlier.

The attack is recorded and logged at 5.05pm. The men were ready to march off at 1100hrs. Why were the men left like sitting ducks, in what's known as 'bomb alley'? Were decisions and debate taking too long as to who, or what was to disembark first? Were communications not right between the echelons of senior officers?

It was clearly a cock up. They had seen the Argentine sky hawks coming down Bomb Alley in Falkland Sound and getting better and better day by day, but the officers argued and could not agree what or who should be unloaded and in what order.

Communication equals control. Without control You have confusion. Which helps the enemy.

Why were the ship and men left for hours in a vulnerable position?

What happened to the so-called land air defence Rapier missiles?

Apparently, they were damaged while being offloaded.

Why was *Sir Galahad* sitting in Fitzroy for five hours? The British force was warned that eight Skyhawks had left the mainland and were making their way to this target. There was no way of passing this on to the ship, or so it is claimed. Incompetence? A carefree attitude? Or both?

This tragic combinations of circumstances was the single largest British loss of life of the campaign. I can now begin to understand why Pierre was furious, and understand how his resentment festered for a very long time. I doubt if we will ever get a really satisfactory, officially revealing explanation but in any case, if it ever appears, it will have come too late for Pierre, who in time, did figure out why the disaster happened but never explained or spoke about it to us.

The air defence were ill prepared for the attack on these men. I begin to understand the resentment felt by Pierre.

According to archival declassified material some 30 years on, this is the official report:

Sir Galahad entered Fitzroy on the 8th June just after 0800hrs local time, to the surprise of some of the Welsh Guards, whose understanding was still that they were being taken directly to Bluff Cove.

Out of the six landing craft that were in the anchorage the day before, four had returned to HMS Intrepid in order to speed the supply situation at San Carlos, one had gone to Goose Green to fetch 5 Brigades sorely needed signals vehicles, and only one, named Foxtrot One, was left unloading the ammunition from Sir Tristram.

There was also a Mexeflote, a kind of powered pontoon raft which was used for unloading stores to the beach, but both this and Foxtrot One were both nearly fully loaded with ammunition crates.

The commanders in charge of unloading the ships at Fitzroy knew that the 350 Welsh Guards had to be off the ship as soon as possible in case of air attack. It was suggested that the Guards could sit on top of the stores on the Mexeflote pontoon and be on shore within the hour.

The Guards Company Commanders were not keen on this as it meant they would have to march 5 miles to Bluff Cove and they were unwilling to weary their men unnecessarily, and all their heavy equipment would have to be left on board, with no guarantee of it being delivered to Bluff Cove in the near future.

A compromise was then reached and the landing craft was made available to run the Guards to Bluff Cove, along with local tractors for the heavy equipment and a local 20 foot cutter.

As this was being discussed, an 846 Squadron Sea King was airlifting the Rapier units ashore, which was to take a total of 18 lifts. Foxtrot One came alongside Sir Galahad at noon in order to start embarking the Welsh Guards, but the Commander of the 16 Field Ambulance, the senior ranking officer there, said that the Guards had already had a chance of disembarking and it was vital that the leading echelon of his unit should have priority.

Twelve men and nine vehicles of the medical unit were then transported ashore which took another hour to do.

On the last trip, the loading ramp of the landing craft was damaged, so the heavy equipment of the Welsh Guards could not be loaded at Sir Galahad stern doors. Instead it was decided that the equipment would be loaded on to the craft by crane, an incredibly slow process, before the men were taken off the ship.

By this time Sir Galahad had been sitting in Fitzroy for five hours, largely due to misunderstandings and a lack of communication.

Sir Tristram had now been unloaded, but was still in the harbour.

Argentinian observation posts on Mount Harriet had been watching the ships and reporting their presence all the time. A reaction was inevitable, eventually eight Skyhawks and six Daggers took off from the mainland and headed towards the ripe target.

The British forces at San Carlos were warned of the raid, probably by a submarine patrolling off Rio Grande, but again due to the communications difficulties the warning did not reach Sir Galahad."

The stage was set for a tragedy.

Three of the Sky hawks and one of the Daggers had to return to base after experiencing technical problems but the rest carried on, going to low level as they approached the islands, the two formations splitting to fly around Lafonia north and south about in order to attack Fitzroy from different directions.

The Dagger formation found HMS Plymouth in Falkland Sound however, steaming to carry out a bombardment of Argentine positions on Mount Rosalie, and decided to attack her.

Plymouth was hit by three bombs, but again the fusing problems of low level releases meant that none exploded. The impact of the bombs detonated a depth charge and started a fire which caused much superficial damage, injuring four men and killing one. One of the Daggers was slightly damaged in the attack.

At Fitzroy the five remaining Skyhawks from Grupo 5 de Caza fell upon the anchorage with almost complete surprise. The units ashore had finally received a warning, but there was no way of passing it to the ships.

The Royal Marine gunners on the ships managed to engage the aircraft, and one Blowpipe shoulder launched missile was fired, but failed to find a target.

Three Skyhawks attacked Sir Galahad and two attacked Sir Tristram. The air defences were ill prepared for this strike; the two Sea Harriers that had formed the Combat Air Patrol to the south were now in pursuit of the Dagger formation and the operational Rapier sites were mainly covering the 5 Brigade Headquarters and the new supply base, not the anchorage. Unfortunately the Rapier site covering the anchorage to the east, the direction from which the Skyhawks attacked, had been damaged in transit and a spare part was just being landed by Sea King as the attack came in.

The tragic combination of circumstance was to cause the single largest British loss of life of the campaign.

Two bombs hit Sir Tristram, one passing straight through the ship without exploding, the other exploding in a small compartment killing two Chinese crewmen.

Sir Galahad suffered far, far worse. Three bombs hit the ship, one passing through a hatch hitting the tank deck, one hitting the engine room and galley and the last burst in the officers' quarters.

The bombs did not explode as the term is commonly understood, they all deflagrated, the casings smashing open on impact, and the contents burning rapidly rather than detonating.

The bomb that hit the tank deck caused most of the casualties, for that was where most of the troops were concentrated, along with twenty tons of ammunition and a large amount of petrol, which became an inferno.

At least forty-five men died on that tank deck, and one hundred and fifty were injured and burned, many of them seriously.

Immediately helicopters came in and started to take the injured off the ship. Foxtrot One was already alongside, protected by the bulk of Sir Galahad from the explosions and began taking wounded on board.

The Mexeflote pontoon also moved in, and some survivors got away on it. Although no one was controlling the rescue, the Sea Kings of 846 and 825 Squadrons, the Wessex from 847 and a Gazelle from 656 Squadrons all cooperated with the surface vessels in perfect harmony.

The wounded were taken at first to the Fitzroy landing site, before a shuttle of helicopters started taking them to Ajax Bay and then on to the hospital ship Uganda, who received 159 casualties this day. Captain Philip Roberts was the last man to leave the ship some forty-five minutes after the attack, which due to the heat of the inferno, was left to burn itself out.

Sir Galahad was towed out to sea later in June and sunk as a war grave.

Forty eight men died in the ship, thirty two of whom were Welsh Guardsmen.

Since then, there have been television documentaries on the Falklands campaign in which the loss of the *Sir Galahad* was prominent and the personal story about Pierre's heroic deeds were featured. Reliving the events as he was interviewed and televised nationally overwhelmed Pierre, and he would break down and recommence some moments later. Recollecting the events was very painful for him. Despite receiving his country's recognition of the part he played, he never felt that it was other than for his comrades and the Royal Army Medical Corps, of which he was a very proud member with its traditions of gallantry shown through time. So strongly did he feel about it that he always remained humble, in fact I don't ever recollect Pierre even wearing his medal, even at events where he was entitled for him to wear it. He hated drawing attention to it.

Pierre was traumatized by the whole experience of war through the sinking of *Sir Galahad*. Nor did he enjoy the regulatory counselling offered by the military and other agencies, to such a degree that, I'm told, he would walk out on such events forced on him. The official advice by the Army is to communicate feelings. He did not want to talk even to his family, let alone divulge personal feelings to any professional counsellors offered.

At this stage in its understanding of the longer-term effects of suffering trauma, the Ministry of Defence appeared not to accept that it existed or to make any attempt to do so when it was clearly evident. We were used to the faraway look in his eyes. Pierre often had "the thousand yards stare" in his eyes, while the acronym 'PTSD' - Post Traumatic Stress Disorder - came into common usage.

The army then did not understand fully or want to accept PTSD. Today PTSD does play a major role in people's lives, although getting those affected by it to articulate pent-up emotions, particularly men who are unused to doing so, is a very difficult long-term process.

Since the Falklands campaign, We have sent thousands of our young men and women to fight in Iraq and Afghanistan. Our society is sitting on a volcano of emotions waiting to erupt in years to come.

The number killed in the Falklands War was 655 Argentinians and 255 British military personnel. The number of suicides of Falklands veterans, as at 2013, outweighs the numbers lost in the fighting – a sobering statistic.

And what has happened to their comrades who failed to come to terms with and remain mentally scarred by what they had done and witnessed "down south", as the islands are known? Their families and veteran associations bear the brunt of their condition and, where there is no one, the worst affected now inhabit the doorways and refuges of the homeless. For many veterans of the conflict, the scars of battle take a long time to heal. Their war does not end when the shooting stops and they return home. They still have a deadly foe to fight, the psychological trauma of their combat experiences. This is something that has been hidden and not fully recognised by the military.

Veterans and their families are still struggling against ignorance and a distinct lack of effective recovery pathways. Those who have sacrificed so much to protect our freedoms deserve our respect and support.

Pierre, on many occasions and anniversaries of the war, was invited by various individuals and agencies to visit the Falkland Islands, together with Nina, on all-expenses-paid trips. He always declined, unable to face the agony and pain again.

Pierre told me of the day he, Nina and Mum went to Buckingham Palace on his Investiture to receive his military medal from Her Majesty The Queen. This is a very special day when an individual who has been awarded an honour receives their award in person from the Queen. About 25 of these are held each year in the Ballroom at Buckingham Palace in London.

He recalled the occasion with great pride. He was admiring all the very rare beautiful paintings and art work hung up along the corridors inside the palace. There, standing alongside him, and also admiring the art work, was a man he vaguely recognised. They exchanged pleasantries and a conversation took place along the lines of "haven't I seen you somewhere before?" It turned out to be the captain of the ill-fated *Sir Galahad*, who had ordered Pierre, as the last man, to jump off the ship on that day in June 1982 in the Falklands. That day, they also stood together on the burning deck of the ship. This was the same naval officer coming out of the thick dense smoke, and the burning *Sir Galahad* ship, gesticulating to Pierre that a helicopter was coming for them.

Pierre lost all his belongings, as did everybody else, when the ship was blown up by the Argentine Skyhawks.

There are very few, if any, authentic photographs or even snaps taken of the event on board, because virtually all cameras were lost in abandoning ship. People set off with cameras but never returned with them.

Pierre also lost his UK passport. This became a very sore point with Pierre because its replacement developed into a major issue. Pierre and I discussed the hassle, anguish and grief he underwent in the UK, to replace his passport. It started badly with a long-winded jargon-jangling letter that Pierre received from the Passport Office. Some bureaucratic twit refused his application for a replacement UK passport, which angered him. The letter went on to add insult to injury by stating he had no right to stay in the UK or claim British Citizenship, let alone be entitled to a replacement passport. Pierre at this particular time was still a serving member in Her Majesty's Armed Forces, and to rub salt in wounds, a decorated Falkland War hero who fought for his country. He was put through the treadmill.

This was a disaster for Pierre. It was more than he could take, but he battled on. He was extremely anxious at the decision and did not know what else he could do.

It was not until three and a half years later that he got a new replacement passport. Pierre was understandably very bitter about this whole affair.

Here is the offending letter from the Passport Office and Foreign and Commonwealth Office Dated 12 January 1983, addressed to Pierre at Princess Alexandra Hospital, RAF Wroughton, Swindon, Wilts. I would like to share it with the readers.

Dear Sir

With reference to your recent letter and passport application, I am sorry to have to tell you that you are no longer eligible for a United Kingdom passport because you ceased to be a citizen of the United Kingdom and Colonies under legislative arrangements made for the independence of Seychelles.

As a citizen of Seychelles, whose citizenship you automatically acquired on the 29 June 1976, you are eligible to apply for a passport to the High Commissioner for Seychelles, 30 Woburn place, London, WC1 OTR.

Whenever a Colonial territory achieves independence, Parliament makes provision in the relevant United Kingdom legislation that any citizen of the United Kingdom and Colonies who derives his citizenship solely from his connection with that territory should, if he becomes a citizen of the new country by operation of law at independence, lose his citizenship of the United Kingdom and Colonies unless he or his father or paternal grandfather was born, naturalised or registered in the United Kingdom or in one of the remaining Colonies.

As you did not come into any of these categories, you ceased to be a citizen of the United Kingdom and Colonies on the 29 June 1976 <u>by operation of law</u>.

I would explain that as you were born in Dar es Salaam, the former Protectorate of Tanzania, you derived your United Kingdom citizenship and retained it on the independence of Tanzania, by reason of your father's birth in the Colony of

Seychelles. As your father and paternal grandfather were born in Seychelles, you became a Citizen of Seychelles since the issue of your previous passport.

You should consult the Home Office about the possibility of acquiring British citizenship under the provisions of the British Nationality Act 1981 by writing to the Nationality Division, Lunar House, Wellesley Road, Croydon, CR9 2BY.

Before taking this course however you may wish to seek the advice of the High Commission for Seychelles as to what effect such action may have upon your citizenship of that country.

Once British citizenship has been acquired, it cannot be revoked simply because an applicant finds it has consequences of which he was unaware at the time.

The last paragraph was underlined by the passport office.

If you acquire British citizenship you will then be eligible for a United Kingdom passport on production of your Certificate of Registration.

Your documents are returned for use by the Home Office.

If you require to travel abroad for any reason before your registration is completed, we would consider granting you a temporary passport in view of these exceptional circumstances.

I am sorry to be the bearer of this bad news, particularly in the circumstances in which your passport was lost. However, this would have been conveyed to you on applying for a new passport when the lost passport expires in May 1984.

Yours faithfully.

Reading it again makes me very angry. Nina and Pierre did everything in their power to get this sorted. They felt very bitter and angry and aggrieved, threatening even to go public through the newspapers over this matter. They wrote to Leon Brittan, the former Conservative Member of Parliament, former member of the European Commission and former Home Secretary of the United Kingdom, and got his naturalisation certificate.

The army at that time did nothing to help Pierre get his passport and correct papers, so he had to travel to Rinteln in Germany, where he was posted in 1984/5 travelling only on his army identity card.

Eventually he had to go in front of Nina's ex-boss, a chief superintendent and lawyer, with his naturalisation certificate, swearing an oath of allegiance on the bible. This took them three and a half years to sort out.

On reflection it seems utterly beyond any understanding that it took three and a half years of anxiety that developed in the country that he had served, fought, bled and bandaged for. It was a class one almighty 'balls up' that did nothing for the reputation of the civil service or the Home Office.

On a more positive note, Pierre received many letters congratulating him on his bravery award of the Military Medal from all quarters, too numerous to list here. However, this one he got from Clarence House dated 11th October 1982.

Queen Elizabeth The Queen Mother has asked me to tell you how delighted she is to learn of the Honours and Awards gained by those serving in the Royal Army Medical Corps in the theatre of operations in the South Atlantic.

The recognition of so many members of the Corps is a source of much pride to the Colonel-in-Chief, and is a sure indication that the splendid traditions of courage, compassion and devotion to duty have been most worthily maintained.

The Queen Mother asks if a message of her warmest congratulations may be conveyed to Sergeant Peter Naya, whose Military Medal was obviously awarded for acts of outstanding courage, and to all others who have received such well-deserved recognition.

This is another, from the Director General Of Army Medical Services, Lieutenant General Sir Alan Reay KBE QHP MB FRCP FRCP (Edin), dated 13th October 1982:

Dear Sergeant Naya

I send you my congratulations on your award of the Military Medal for your brave conduct in the Falkland Islands campaign. In particular your gallantry and dedication to duty at the time of the bombing of "Sir Galahad" undoubtedly saved many lives and was in the finest traditions of our Corps.

I have today heard from our Colonel in Chief, Queen Elizabeth The Queen Mother, and she specifically asks that her warmest congratulations be conveyed to you.

We are all extremely proud of you.
Yours sincerely, Alan Reay.

Pierre was extremely proud to think that the writers, many of whom were unknown to him, had taken the time and trouble to set pen to paper with their congratulations and thanks. That from Clarence House made him especially so. These letters have been reproduced here by the kind permission of his widow Nina.

Mrs Patricia Margaret Nutbeem was the wife of the Second-in-Command of 16 Field Ambulance RAMC, Major Roger Nutbeem, RAMC, who was killed on the Sir Galahad. She gained the award of the Most Excellent Order of the British Empire (Civilian) for her unstinted devotion and support to the Unit Wives and families during the Falklands War.

She held regular and frequent meetings of the Wives' Club, which she had founded, and also visited them in the Aldershot area. She wrote to those outside the area. By doing so, she relieved many anxieties and solved domestic problems which arise when soldiers serve on active service.

On the death of her husband and despite caring for her own two children, she actively supported the families of those killed and visited the families of those wounded. This in addition to her Club activities. Her behaviour, one of immense courage in view of her tragic loss, showed as an outstanding example in preserving the morale of the young wives of the Unit. Wives of servicemen on active service away from home are so adept at finding things to do or organising events. This takes their minds elsewhere, even if only for a few hours a day, instead of sitting around worrying about husbands and loved ones.

Some few weeks later, on Pierre's return from the Falklands War, we had a ceremonial regimental dinner in Pierre's honour in the Warrant Officers' and Sergeants' Mess at the Cambridge Military hospital in Aldershot. What a very proud occasion for Pierre to be honoured for his Military Medal award amongst his comrades and other members of his beloved RAMC. The regimental mess was packed full, all dressed in our ceremonial dress.

I was seated very close to him and feeling extremely proud. It was a very emotional evening, especially when the Regimental Sergeant Major read out his citation on his award for Bravery In The Field. There was a rapturous applause from all present. A night to remember.

Cleaning up the Falklands

It fell to the army health team to make the island tolerably habitable after the fighting finished and the Argentinian prisoners had been repatriated. It was not a clean sheet. In fact, it was a very dirty one, and although most of the immediate issues could be cleared, some longer-term ones could not be tackled and resolved completely. Here I would like to paint a picture of some of the problems facing the team and the sterling work done by it.

The administration control cell was to be responsible for the welfare, including the sanitary provisions, of an expected ten thousand prisoners of war, to be held in selected areas on the Falklands. However, much of this anticipated activity was pre-empted by the rapid repatriation of the bulk of the Argentine prisoners of war. In many aspects this represented a welcome reprieve from what would have been a most difficult task in an extremely inhospitable environment with insufficient essential resources.

Consequently, the health team was now in a position to direct its attention towards the environmental health problems now facing those in the capital, Port Stanley, and other civilian settlements and military locations throughout the islands.

Due to the inevitable breakdown in public utilities the civilian refuse collection service had failed, leaving a huge mess in Stanley and the surrounding area. Refuse, rotting food, weapons, ammunition and the debris of war were scattered indiscriminately throughout the town. The clean-up began with the team organising prisoners to collect refuse into organised piles. During the next three to four weeks this rough refuse collection developed to involve the civilian collection agency, which restored a sense of order and normality to the town.

The municipal refuse tip was in a deplorable state. All classes of refuse had to be tipped indiscriminately over the entire site. A number of fires had to be started on the tip but, as most refuse contained a significant proportion of live ammunition, grenades etc., tip maintenance became an unusually hazardous experience for the army health team.

The tip face overlooked the sea and the remaining tip perimeter was bounded by an Argentine mine field, so it was not possible to expand the tipping area to cope with the increased refuse burden. The sheer volume of refuse produced continued to make life difficult, so a second tip was created using heavy equipment from the army engineers.

While this clean-up was making steady progress, the civilian water and purification and distribution systems were functioning erratically and at a level which could not be relied upon to produce a potable public water supply. This presented the health team with another task. In an attempt to satisfy the needs of the military garrison, engineers had set up and were running a number of water points in the area. It was winter in the Falklands and the freezing temperatures there affected the field water purification equipment that required much attention to maintain supply.

The civilian water purification plant had been shelled during the battle for the liberation of Port Stanley. It was not running well and was unable to produce drinkable water. Extensive repair and replacement works were necessary.

As the volume of water was insufficient to satisfy the combined needs of the civilian and military population, strict water rationing was introduced. In the event of that not being enough, instructions were issued and broadcast advising everyone to boil or otherwise sterilise all water for human consumption. Radio broadcasts on the local network continued to inform islanders about health concerns.

As many of the civilian population of Port Stanley as could do so had moved to the settlements to try to escape the troubles. When they began to return to their homes, this simply added to the problems faced by the authorities. It became apparent that many of the dwellings that had been occupied by the Argentines had been damaged and often grossly fouled with human excrements and spoilt by their unwelcome guests.

The Argentines had occupied many public buildings, warehouses and schools. They had left these in a deplorable and often unhygienic condition. As well as the indiscriminate and thoughtless disposal of human excrement and general refuse in them, extensive supplies of food, including meat in varying stages of decomposition, were continually being uncovered, making the urgent, efficient disposal and cleaning a priority.

This clean-up was an added call upon the limited water available, which restricted progress. Without clean water a modern developed society can achieve little in maintaining the fight against filth, vermin and disease.

The re-establishment of communities followed quickly and the forces found better accommodation in church halls and warehouses.

By mid-July it was clear that there had been much progress, despite winter conditions, in the control of refuse and waste disposal, the provision of potable water supply and the cleaning of available accommodation. The army brought in extra generators and the old electricity distribution system was largely restored. A series of well-coordinated major rodent campaigns was instigated. Many valuable liaison links were forged with both service and civilian agencies.

All but 1000 of the prisoners of war had been moved from the Falklands, and those remaining were held in two groups of equal size. Those in Port Stanley were accommodated in the warehouses and workshops and were employed in mine clearance tasks and the clearing up of the town. They were also made primarily responsible for the burial of their own dead soldiers. The remaining prisoners, all senior officers, were accommodated in a disused meat refrigeration plant at Ajax Bay, once the location of Pierre's field hospital.

The variety and quality of living accommodation occupied by service personnel presented the army health environmentalists with numerous problems. It was very cold. Tents were in very short supply. Troops were housed in domestic properties, warehouses, school halls, churches, sheds, outhouses and improvised shelters, in fact anywhere that provided some cover against the winter weather.

The general standard of accommodation was extremely poor. However, ingenuity, coupled with building skills, saw many shanty-type dwellings converted into reasonable windproof and weatherproof living spaces.

An answer to this problem was provided by the gathering and anchoring of vessels within the inner harbour of Port Stanley, to be used as accommodation ships. They made a motley collection which included ferries, a container ship and the hastily-refurbished RFA *Sir Tristram*. This ship had suffered bomb damage during the Bluff Cove incident during which the *Sir Galahad* was destroyed.

The sleeping facilities aboard such craft were considered satisfactory, if somewhat crowded. The public rooms aboard the car ferries had areas for rest and relaxation which *Sir Tristram* sadly lacked.

In none of the ships were sanitary and ablution facilities really sufficient to cope with the numbers and, almost needless to say, sewage treatment plants were severely strained.

The need for troops to launder clothing regularly, due to the extremely dirty working conditions encountered at many of the civilian engineering project sites, also created difficulties. Some laundry facilities and washing machines were provided, but not on the scale required to cope with the task.

Catering hygiene, food storage and preparation presented another area of concern. In general the galleys were designed to produce snack-type meals for short-haul passengers and could not cope effectively with the demands of producing up to a thousand meals per sitting for hungry, fit soldiers. A system of staggered meal times was instigated, but while this eased the problems of meal preparation, it left little time to cope with a worsening food hygiene problem.

Adding to this the real concern about the inability of the accommodation ships to make enough drinking water to meet the needs of the embarked personnel, there was a probability that gastrointestinal illness of some sort would break out on board. The most common 'bug' to strike the penned in servicemen caused a gastrointestinal upset of notoriety which lasted 24-48 hours and became dubbed locally "Galtieri's Revenge". In an attempt to avert this, a programme of routine deep cleaning in such complexes was initiated by the army health team.

The storage and disposal of refuse in connection with accommodation ships represented another area of concern. While these car ferries were operating on their normal British Channel routes, refuse could be stored for discharge at the point of disembarkation. In the Falklands this option was not possible. Nor was it possible to discharge refuse and swill directly into the sea, as the ships were permanently at anchor within the inner harbour.

To compound the difficulties, remember that these vessels were sitting in a shallow, almost enclosed anchorage, into which the sewage effluent from the ships themselves had to be discharged. In addition, no sewage treatment or purification takes place in Port Stanley and the town's raw sewage is continually discharged into the inner harbour. There is, therefore, the ever-present risk of grossly-contaminated water gaining access to the water storage tanks on ships, or into the osmosis plants used to purify the water used on board should any of them fail. Not a safe place to go for a midnight swim. A number of options in respect of refuse disposal were investigated. The method chosen reduced handling and transfer operations to a minimum, and worked well.

The garbage was loaded aboard a captured Argentine tug, which tied up alongside each of the principal accommodation ships, every other day. Once loaded the tug would carry the refuse well out to sea and then discharge it in a manner and location that would minimise nuisance.

A major cause of concern in connection with the accommodation ships was their inability to make sufficient water of acceptable quality to satisfy the needs of embarked personnel. Water rationing became a common feature of life aboard ship.

The Falkland Islands climate can at best be described as unpredictable. It must surely be one of the few areas in the world where one can experience all four seasons in a day.

The islands are situated in the South Atlantic at 52 degrees latitude south, which relates closely to the position of UK in the northern hemisphere, but that is where the similarity ends. They lie in the path of the West Wind Drift and therefore under the influence of the cold icy seas of the Antarctic and incessant westerly air currents. The winter brings with it wind speeds over 50mph with gusts of up to 90 mph in exposed locations.

In all campaigns of this nature, sickness rates and manpower wastage due to disease are a concern. Fortunately no major epidemics occurred and no exotic diseases were diagnosed. The general health of the local population remained good.

Once the troops of the Task Force landed on the islands they had to march over mountainous and wet boggy terrain in the face of driving rain and extreme cold. It was expected that cold weather casualties would occur. In fact many cases of trench foot were reported, with mild discolouration of the feet and swelling causing walking difficulty. Little information is available about the incidence of frostbite, but a few cases did occur.

Dhahran and Desert Storm

Pierre completed his military service in the Royal Army Medical Corps with the rank of Staff Sergeant after serving for 22 years. He did so a couple of years before I took my leave of the same Corp after 23 years in 1989.

He went on to serve in the National Health Service in hospital management, looking after sterile supplies units providing sterile instrumentation for hospital operating theatres for a few more years before retiring from work and leaving to start a new life in the Portuguese Algarve. He bought and started to renovate a beautiful town house within the ancient walled city of Lagos. This work took him and Nina a few years to complete, with startling results. They were very proud of their work.

His love of the sea and boats, nurtured all those years ago growing up in East Africa, saw him attending night school to learn navigational skills and seamanship, culminating in him getting his small boat skipper's licence, which is no mean achievement.

My Hong Kong posting in the late 80s was one of the last I would complete while in the Armed Forces. I left the army with the rank of Warrant Officer and continued in the medical field by working in hospital management, also involved in supplying surgical instrumentation for operating theatres. I also worked as a freelance operating theatre technician in theatres across the United Kingdom for a few years. Travelling back and forth to assignments from my Hereford home proved arduous. I was hardly at home, and very tired when I was.

Variety being the spice of life, I also worked for a period of time as a medic on the oil and gas drilling rigs in the North Sea, Norwegian waters, and further afield. My last position was on a diving vessel, looking after the divers exploring the ocean depths of the cold North Sea. This specially-built diving ship was a particularly interesting assignment. The ship was equipped with two hyperbaric chambers which could hold nine divers for periods up to twenty-eight days. My responsibility on board as the medic was to look after the divers in the hyperbaric chambers as well as the other 200 associated personnel on board the vessel. Effectively I was the first line in providing medical cover.

These chambers are most associated with treating divers with decompression sickness, the bends, which may occur if they return to the surface too quickly, resulting in nitrogen bubbles forming in their blood. As a diver descends, nitrogen, which makes up about 80% of the air, is absorbed into the body's tissues. If a diver ascends slowly, the nitrogen slowly seeps out of the body's tissues and is exhaled in a process called off gassing. However if a diver ascends too quickly without ample time to 'off gas', nitrogen forms tiny bubbles in the blood, and causes sufferers to bend and contort, giving the decompression sickness its colloquial name 'the bends'.

If a diver gets the 'bends' seriously while resurfacing, he is quickly placed in a chamber and repressurised, after which the chamber pressure is reduced very slowly to mimic a slow ascent. This process will be under the control of the attending medic to ensure the diver's safety.

Although I did have to attend special medic training for this type of work, I found this assignment, with all its responsibilities, highly stressful.

I committed a cardinal sin in 1991 while working as a manager in Hereford NHS hospital. I volunteered to serve my country.

It was an action completely contrary to all my 23 years' training in the army, which decrees that you do not volunteer for anything, under any circumstances. But I volunteered to be a medic and would be involved in the first gulf war in Operation Desert Storm.

The need for medical personnel, especially highly-trained Operating Theatre Technicians, to volunteer to return to service temporarily arose because the Army Medical Corps had started a programme of reducing the number of experienced servicemen, like myself and Pierre, to reduce running costs. This had created a shortage of operating theatre technicians to fulfil the commitment to man fully several field hospitals in the Gulf region.

I was posted to a small, highly mobile, seventy-bedded medical support troop in the town of Dhahran, a very large airbase in Saudi Arabian. The design of this mobile field hospital used the concept of collective protection technology. In practice the whole hospital resembled a blown-up tent, made out of parachute-type material and pressurized by generators pumping clean, filtered air into the different compartments to prevent the ingress of any nuclear, biological and chemical agents. The idea is that those inside the tent can work unimpeded by the wearing of respirators. This was, at that time, a revolutionary technology, used by the British Army Medical Services and the envy of the world's military armies.

The Americans did not have this facility available, and used specially-built, fully-equipped containers, airlifted from USA, as operating theatres. As a result, they had to constantly wear personal respirators when working. I know which one I would choose to work under.

Our role was to provide medical support to the airbase, as well as being the centre for vaccinations and the well-being of troops stationed there. We were also a mobile unit and were ready to move at very short notice to anywhere in the Gulf, should this be necessary.

The vaccinations programme was in my opinion very controversial. The military authorities did not know exactly what chemical warfare substances Saddam Hussein might release on our troops. They were, therefore, subject to a concoction of vaccinations protecting them against anthrax, plague and cholera, the side effects of which played hell with some chaps then and, reportedly for years to come.

Anaphylactic shock occurred in several people, with blackouts, unconsciousness and severe headaches for days after. I witnessed big, strapping, fit soldiers just collapsing on being vaccinated. Naps tablets had to be taken daily, as this is the antidote and pre-treatment to combat some chemical weapons.

All these competing vaccines were given in a single session. We were exposed to heavy use of pesticides and organophosphates, over which there are many serious safety questions. We were also later exposed to atmospheric pollution from burning oil wells.

There was a possibility of exposure to nerve agents, or so we were informed at the time. Within our complex there was a medical research unit tent, from the research unit at Porton Down in the UK, where experiments on chemicals are carried out, loaded with test tubes, and paraphernalia associated with what looked like a laboratory. Needless to say this was a strictly restricted area and totally out of bounds to all other personnel.

I clearly remember the day the oil wells were set on fire. It was a normal bright sunny day, but we could see a huge black cloud descending on to our area, slowly turning day turned into night.

The Ministry of Defence will not identify Gulf War Syndrome and its existence. This is a multi-symptom disorder affecting returning military veterans. A wide range of acute and chronic illness have been linked to it. It is not to be confused with PTSD.

It was during this period that John Major, who had just been made Prime Minister, came out to the Gulf to visit us. I managed to get to shake his hand and got a lovely photograph to go with it. I later sent this to 10 Downing Street, and he duly obliged with his signature. I have it still, as a memento of that period in my life.

Part of my job was to line the troops up outside the vaccination tent awaiting their jabs. To date I still have my atropine antidote chemical injection syrette in my emergency respirator bag in the loft and my photo with John Major in the hallway of my house. Don't ask me why I still keep it - the atropine I mean of course.

The chilling sound of air raid sirens was frequently heard both day and night. Dhahran is situated between Iraq in the north and the Saudi Arabian capital Riyadh, so consequently, the radar systems would pick up activity of the Iraqi fired scud missiles aimed at that city and others.

The American Patriot anti-missile defence system was fully operational on the airbase and elsewhere in the Gulf region. The Patriot system has a remarkable goal. It is designed to detect, target and then hit an incoming missile that may be no more than ten to twenty feet long, and is typically flying at three to five times the speed of sound. An upgraded version can also destroy incoming aircraft and cruise missiles.

The Patriot missile system has been deployed in many situations. It is able to shoot down enemy Scud missiles and protect soldiers and civilians from such an attack.

Patriot missile batteries were activated several times in the Iraqi war and were used extensively in the 1991 Gulf War. A Patriot missile depends on ground-based radar to find, identify and track its target. An incoming missile could be fifty miles away when the Patriot's radar locks onto it. At this distance, the incoming missile would not even be visible to a human being, much less identifiable. It is even possible for the Patriot system to operate in a completely automatic mode with no human intervention at all.

An incoming missile flying at Mach 5 is travelling approximately one mile every second. There is little time to react and respond once the enemies missile is detected, making automatic detection and launching an important feature.

Since a Patriot missile battery can have up to sixteen launchers, and there are also spare missiles to resupply the launchers as missiles are fired, you can see that deploying a Patriot is very expensive and is not a small endeavour.

An equipment van known as the Engagement Control Station (ECS) houses an array of computers and consoles to control the battery. Each launcher is roughly the size of a tractor trailer rig, as is the ECS and the power supply truck.

There are also highly-trained operating personnel, technicians, support personnel, fuel for the generators, security forces to protect the battery.

I remember one particular night when a patriot missile was activated. General alarm sounded immediately. Unfortunately, it chose to destroy the incoming Scud missile without exploding the warhead, which with other debris, fell on to the next sleeping quarter a few hundred yards away from where I was billeted. The sky above us was illuminated like a fireworks display and a thunderous bang.

Many of the occupants of the barracks, a corrugated-metal warehouse that had been converted into temporary housing for the newly arrived American troops, who were eating dinner or relaxing when the missile warhead dropped on them. Others were apparently working out or sleeping, as many survivors wandered around wounded and dazed, in sweat suits or gym shorts, looking stunned during the rescue efforts.

Chaos engulfed the scene after the burning debris fell into the converted warehouse. Saudis in the neighbourhood followed its fall from the sky and quickly ran to the scene, complicating rescue efforts and creating a chaotic scene.

In the most devastating Iraqi strike of the Persian Gulf war, a Scud missile demolished the barrack block accommodating more than 100 American troops, killing 27 and wounding 98. The gigantic explosion, 100 feet off the ground, was followed by another, as bits of glowing metal fell to the ground setting fire to the barracks, which was situated in Al Khobar, a city a few miles from Dhahran. The building caught fire at once. Within an hour, it was a charred skeleton. If the Scud missile had missed, even by yards, it would have landed harmlessly into the desert waste land surrounding the barracks.

All casualties were taken by ambulance to local civilian hospitals in the area. None came to our establishment. I was extremely lucky to be alive that night. As the American CNN network covered the war instantly on live television broadcasts, news of this disaster had already arrived in the UK, so urgent phone calls were made to families back home to reassure them of our safety.

When the war was over we were requested, for logistical reasons, to pack the whole field hospital and set it alight, as it was decreed that the material had lost its integrity in the hot Saudi Arabian sun. What a waste!

The American troops' ration packs were known as MRE, which stands for Meal Ready to Eat, and were the main individual operational ration for the U.S. military. We nicknamed them Meals Rejected by Ethiopians, which made the Yanks laugh. MREs are meant to be completely self-contained, flexibly-packed meals that provide all the nutrition a soldier on the go needs to sustain himself. Typical contents would include entrée, side dish, crackers, peanut butter, cheese spread dessert, instant coffee, toilet paper and a heater to heat the main entrée.

It was all reconstituted food, similarly to that which the astronauts ate on their missions. While everything in an MRE can be eaten cold, it usually tastes better warmed up, although I found it horrible.

The Yanks hated their own rations, so they came frequently to our camp for a food swap. They loved our British substantial compo rations, which were packed inside a small cardboard box with enough retort pouched and canned foods to feed one soldier for 24 hours. These, also known as the 24-hour ration packs, were available in seven menus that provided two precooked meals, breakfast and main meal, plus a midday snack.

The war was short-lived and I returned to my job in Hereford Hospital a few months later. My return was short-lived too, as I found a couple of weeks later that the hospital management had made me redundant from my position.

All in all, not a good time in life. The promise by the Ministry of Defence, which assured personnel going to the Gulf that their jobs would be secure, turned out, for me, to be so much hot air. So much for job protection while serving your country. I was a very angry soldier.

While I was seriously considering volunteering for the Gulf War, Pierre had been absolutely distraught at the possibility that I might go to war against Saddam Hussein. He begged me not to go, but I did not listen to my veteran brother, although he had experienced the real trauma of war. He did not want me to endure what he had had to fight through. With hindsight, I wish I had listened to him, especially having to put my family and himself through the pain and anguish of yet another war.

Turtles and tuna

In 2000, Pierre, his wife Nina, myself and my wife Barbara, my younger brother Andy and his wife Valerie, decided to go on a holiday to the Seychelles Islands and briefly visit Dar es Salaam en route. I felt truly elated by the prospect of visiting the birthplace of our father in the Seychelles, the home of his family for generations. Although Mum was born in Mombasa, Kenya, several generations of her family also came from the exotic Seychelles. The whole holiday promised to be a treat for us.

It was really a nostalgic trip tinged also with many memories and sadness as we had lost our mother six years earlier on the 26th April 1994. She died in Colchester Hospital while awaiting a leg amputation, due to diabetes and associated illness. This was also after losing our father some 26 years previously.

The visit to see our own birthplace with our wives left us very sad - and annoyed. In Tanzania we saw how the beautiful country we had left many years before had deteriorated so much so quickly. It was virtually unrecognisable, with the collapse of infrastructure and the rise of shanty towns everywhere you looked. Where once stood lush countryside, the places we met in, played in and fished from had been overrun, and our memories of them were the only mementos left for us.

There was a population explosion taking place. Every man and his dog wanted to come into the city from outlying villages, living in makeshift shanty huts constructed out of cardboard, or any materials they could lay their hands on. Roads and pavements were virtually non-existent.

We were all saddened to the point of despair. All familiar landmarks, many buildings and houses had gone, producing an impression of a scene from Mad Max the movie. Now with over four million inhabitants from all walks of life, Dar es Salaam had become a very different place from the one we had found so enjoyable in our youth.

The reasons for this growth and population explosion are the same for cities all over the world - population growth and the possibility of a better lifestyle. While the city remains the country's commercial hub, everyone is struggling to find a living, and with that, crime has moved in. Most of the pavements along city roads are an eyesore, with many stalls awash with all sorts of merchandise during the day. At night they are turned into shelter for homeless vendors and hideouts for petty criminals.

Previous administrations in the city attempted to remove street vendors and relocate them to assigned spaces, but this was short lived. The Machinga complex at Mchikichini area in Ilala district is one such location for the small traders to display and sell their wares. We were told that space allocation at the complex was riddled with corruption, with the result that the small traders were forced back on to the city pavements in increasing numbers. High rates of unemployment, coupled with harsh living conditions in rural areas aggravated the influx of youth to the cities, including Dar es Salaam. Now the city pavements are overcrowded with stalls, putting the lives of pedestrians at risk as they have to walk on the roads.

Apart from traffic risks, the city is awash with filth and garbage in many areas. Their recycling programme is non-existent, and the people need to be persuaded that this is a severe health problem. No wonder Dar es Salaam has been mentioned among the dirtiest cities in the world, despite efforts to keep it clean. It now has the nickname 'Dar es Slum'.

In the Seychelles we booked ourselves a touch of luxury in one of the beach chalets in Anse Royale, a lovely location just a few miles outside Mahe, the capital. The chalets were all just the width of the beach from the sea, one of the beaches of the Seychelles that are widely considered as some of the most spectacular in the world.

It was difficult to draw ourselves away from the spectacular view we had to visit other local islands like La Digue and Praslin, which were just as breathtakingly attractive. Indeed, so beautiful was Praslin that it was once thought to be the original sight of the Garden of Eden.

The legendary Vallée de Mai on Praslin is where the wondrously-shaped coco-de-mer nut grows high on ancient palms. This was the backdrop of beautiful tropical flowers and plants that both Pierre and myself loved and tried to emulate and nurture in our later lives.

My life as a gardener has grown from these beautiful surroundings and I now realise where I got the drive and passion for horticulture. Pierre always loved and grew many species of plants, especially the exotic types of cannas and dahlias.

One early evening, on our strip of Anse Royale beach, overlooked by our chalet, we watched silently as a large green turtle appeared at the water's edge, going up and down along the shoreline looking for the exact spot to come on the beach to lay her eggs. Weighing up to 700 pounds, green turtles are among the largest sea turtles in the world. Their proportionately small head is non-retractable and extends from a heart-shaped carapace that measures up to five feet. Males are slightly larger than females and have a longer tail. Both have flippers that resemble paddles, which make them powerful and graceful swimmers.

We moved away slightly as this majestic animal drew herself up the sandy beach towards some leafy undergrowth, where she dug a hole and laid her eggs. It was a huge effort for her to do so, but it provided another magical memory for us.

They say that turtles return to the same very beach where they were hatched to lay their own eggs, in their thousands. Green turtles, like other sea turtles, undertake lengthy migrations from feeding sites to nesting grounds, normally on sandy beaches. Mating occurs every two to four years and normally takes place in shallow waters close to the shore. To nest, females leave the sea and choose an area, often on the same very beach used by their mothers, to lay their eggs. They dig a pit in the sand with their flippers, fill it with a clutch of 100 to 200 eggs, cover the pit and return to the sea, leaving the eggs to hatch, which takes about two months.

The most dangerous time of a green turtle's life is when it makes the journey from nest to sea. Many predators, including crabs and flocks of gulls, voraciously prey on hatchlings during this short scamper. We kept that story away from the locals, although I feel sure they knew for themselves. The turtles are still killed for their meat and eggs. Their numbers are also reduced by boat propeller accidents, fishnets, which drown them, and the destruction of their nesting grounds by human encroachment.

This holiday was a time when Pierre looked at his happiest and normal chirpy self, probably because he was looking forward to the fishing trips. We had very distant relatives and close friends living and working in the Seychelles. They were fanatical, knowledgeable and talented line fishermen, with modern equipment.

We chartered a luxurious very well equipped skippered boat with seating for eight. The leader of our expedition was a relative, and we made up the number fishing with three seasoned friends, all of whom were competition fishermen. They fished regularly on the island and won numerous fishing competitions, in which many competitors from all parts of the world took part.

There was excitement in Pierre's eyes as we set out in the morning in good conditions. Our friends, of course, knew all the best fishing spots and could guide the skipper perched high on the boat in the control cabin, straight to them with their hand held GPS system. The result was that we had a never-to be-forgotten day's fishing. This was stuff of boys, dreams, recalling our times of fishing off Dar's rocks and from our little boat *Souflette* that Pop had built, only this time we did not have to prepare lines, hooks, baits and all the associated paraphernalia. It was all laid on for us.

What a day that turned out to be after an early start, collecting dry ice to chill any fish that we might be lucky enough to catch. Large igloo ice boxes were already on board filled with essential victuals to keep us in the mood, including the local Seychellois beer 'Sey Brew'. This was definitely a boy's day out when Pierre, Andy and I joined the others at the marina, also intent on making it an exciting day.

Samed, a local businessman, owned a fish restaurant in town and was married to my cousin Lloy's daughter, an ex-Miss Seychelles and very pretty indeed. Lloy played the percussion in Pierre's 'Blue Shadows' band many years ago in Dar. Samed was obviously looking for a good day's catch for his restaurant and was joined by two of his fishing friends, who, it transpired, were very experienced competition fishermen. One of them was a very young-looking Seychellois who, in conversation, declared he was a jumbo jet pilot for Air Seychelles.

The skipper was a very capable man and he had organised all the gear for the day's fishing, although Pierre, a skipper himself, kept an eye on proceedings, and was in his element enquiring about the array of rods and reels and paraphernalia of fishing.

It seemed only a short time later that, at the speed we were making, we lost sight of Mahe, some 30 km behind us. We powered towards the fishing ground, skimming over the calm surface of a sea unruffled by any breeze except what the boat's speed generated, leaving a stream of waves and surf from the high-powered engines trailing behind.

As I write this, piracy is an ever-present threat in the area we were heading for, but fortunately there was no risk at that time to our enjoyment of the whole occasion, nor did this influence our trip of a lifetime, fishing in our fatherland.

Meanwhile, the rods, reels and lures were prepared and laid out. Rods were put into their respective rod holders on the boat and the two outriggers, one on each side of the boat were prepared to be deployed.

Samed navigated by the hand-held GPS system, constantly checking its readings until he thought we had reached the fishing grounds. Times had changed since those times in our youth in Dar es Salaam, when Pop used only landmarks and intuition to guide us to those jealously-guarded fishing grounds he preferred.

The techniques used by these guys on board were tried and tested over many previous fishing trips, and competitions held on the islands. Samed, like Pop, closely guarded his prized fishing hotspots in the Seychelles islands.

The waters of the Seychelles islands are warm and crystal clear, with no pollution of any description, and deserve their description as 'the paradise islands of this world', having an abundance of all species of fish.

In the calm, warm, crystal-clear sea, having sampled just a little of the delights of the chill boxes, now was the time to set about the business of the day, fishing. This was to be the real excitement. This was game fishing on 50lb breaking strain lines, each with several large hooks and lures trailing behind the boat. Some four 50lb breaking strain nylon lines each held an array of lures in different styles and shapes and colours and with seven to eight large hooks paced along the lines. The hooks were no smaller than six inches in length.

These lines were trawled behind the boat at no more than 30 metres or so distance. Other rods and lines, also with lures of different shapes that mimicked fish in distress, were deployed at a further distance, some sixty or more metres further behind.

The boat's speed was reduced to entice the fish to take the hook. Our target here was the yellowfin tuna, which would also be the source of ground fishing bait at a later stage of the fishing expedition.

First we had to find where fish were present, so each person on board would be on high alert for sightings of activity. This was not the time for idle chitchat. This was high-tech big game fishing. It was a tense period. The skipper, perched on high in his viewing point, would be scanning the horizon and the rest of us would also be looking out for bird or gull activity, unusual large ripples on the surface or disturbance on the very calm sea surface that would indicate fish feeding and activity near the surface.

Yellowfin tuna feed near the surface of the sea and can grow to a large size. Their muscular, streamlined torpedo shape makes them very fast, aggressive swimmers. The colours can also be tinged with blue markings, making them an attractive species.

We were very soon in luck. I use that term, because in fishing it's about your luck on the day that counts. Fish disturbance was spotted as the boat, with its engines just purring, manoeuvred into the area and immediately we were in action. The four short lines would be straining at the leash as some three to four fish took the hooks on each line.

The lines were immediately hauled on board with tuna in the region of two-three feet long in all their magical colours of yellow and blue. Fish flapping all around our feet were soon dispatched into the storage boxes with glee. Smiles were on everybody's faces, not least Pierre's. His cheeky grin had returned.

The lines were very quickly deployed again, and the boat made another sweep of the area and followed the telltale signs on the surface, which now appeared to be a frenzy of activity. We were in the fish zone. Each pull of the four lines would produce in the region of four to five fish, some even more. This continued for several sweeps of the area. This was a very new experience for us compared to, in our earlier days, fishing with Pop in the seas around Dar es Salaam all those years ago. What joy and excitement!

We soon had some forty-odd fish, all yellowfin tuna. At the time we did not realise the guys with us were actually fishing for groundbait for later on, and did not find the very salty flavour of the flesh to their taste.

We did not have long to wait, before the much bigger and more highly prized sailfish were now taking the longer lines with bigger lures and hooks that measured around a foot long. All the reels had clutches which were expertly tensioned for when the large fish took the line. There was an obvious tug and bend in the rod, before you handled it.

Ask any fisherman and he will tell you that the most exhilarating moment in any fishing trip is the 'take', when a fish takes the baited hook at the end of your line, makes a run for it and the strike is made. Once a large fish was on the hook, the rod bent to 45 degrees, and one person would be delegated to reel the fish aboard. All other rods and lines were reeled into the boat simultaneously, allowing you all the space and mobility.

At certain times the huge sailfish, some two metres long, would break the surface and sail through the air for twenty yards, violently shaking and bucking, trying to dislodge the hook from its jaws. What a majestic and thrilling sight. This was exhilarating stuff and definitely not the place to be without knowing immediately what to do.

Great activity and professionalism immediately took place on board when a large fish was hooked. The skipper's job was to watch the catch and vary the boat's speed to stay with it, to allow the fisherman to control and reel in the fish. His skill was essential in succeeding to land the fish.

The golden rule these guys applied was to fish only with 50lb breaking strain lines. This enabled them to claim any record when the fish was weighed on returning to the island.

As a precaution against the fish biting through the line in its attempt to break free, the hooks are attached to the line through a leader, a short section of heavier line. Once the fish was hooked, it had to be played, during which time the line had to be kept taut while still allowing the fish to run and then be reeled in as its strength ebbed and it became easier for the fisherman to draw the fish to the side of the boat. This was extremely strenuous and could take as long as half an hour. The gillie, with a gloved hand, would reach out and grab the leader line, at the same time gaffing the fish and pulling it aboard. This was the most dangerous time for everyone, as the fish tried its best to get away with its last despairing lunge for freedom. Sailfish have very long pointed beaks and razor-sharp teeth, so everyone had to be very alert and careful.

It was a messy business. The fish was dispatched with a couple of blows to its head with a wooden truncheon and hauled into the storage boxes so that fishing could start again very quickly. There was blood everywhere, through the use of the gaff and truncheon.

The fish were attracted by the vibrations in the water. These were created by the boat's engines and by lures of all shapes and sizes. Some of these would cost upwards of £50 each, so it was expensive if any were lost through line breakage, as one or two were.

Sweat pouring down your face and into your eyes from the exertion of both fishing and then hauling the catch aboard made seeing very uncomfortable in the salty sea spray. Handling a rod with a catch on was a two-handed job so there had to be someone with a towel handy.

All this effort and excitement provoked a good appetite and lunch was a welcome relief. It was served with freshly-caught tuna and rice, washed down with the local Seychellois beer - delicious.

Pierre was treasuring this experience and had a big smile every time you looked at him. Again his luck held and it was he who caught the first and biggest sailfish of the day. In all we caught in the region of eight large sailfish, barracudas and kingfish, all delicacies. We had luck with us that day.

Lunch over, the next stage of this great day took us to the ground fishing for red snappers and groupers. All the rods and trawling lines were reeled in and stowed. Some of the tuna we had caught earlier were now being prepared as bait. The look on our faces was aghast with disbelief when the gillie started gutting and throwing away all the horrible intestines and things, then slicing huge pieces of tuna steak, a size that would fill a large plate in a fish restaurant. We must have been looking to catch big fish.

After moving a short distance away using GPS guidance, we found ourselves handline fishing. This was the style of fishing we had done as teenagers with Pop in Dar es Salaam all those years ago. We were in our element.

The huge steaks of tuna were put on two or three large hooks about nine inches in length. The line was weighted with what seemed around one kilo in lead, tied at the end of the line and long enough to reach to the sea bed. This time the line was made of cord, and not nylon. We were in very deep water with strong currents.

When a fish was felt to be taking the bait, the line was jerked tight and then relaxed. This was repeated two or three times and only when the fisherman was satisfied he had hooked something would he begin to haul in his anticipated catch.

At one stage I was handed the line to pull in and I was immediately in trouble as I struggled. To me it felt like hauling in a 25-kilo sack of potatoes. I found myself pulling up three large red snappers two or three feet long, each weighing what felt a ton on one single line. There was no feeling of the fish moving on the line. These fish were huge enough to be served buffet-style in hotels and restaurants, spiced and grilled Seychellois Creole style. They are the best tasting fish to be found in the Seychelles.

When we stopped fishing that day, we had about a dozen red snappers in the cold boxes. What a delicious, and for Samed, a lucrative, prospect they offered for his restaurant in the town centre! However, at this point the day was coming to an end and it was time to head back to Mahe and the mainland.

What happened next started with the last cast of the day, which was retrieved with just half a fish on the hook. Instantly we knew we had a hungry shark nosing around, muscling in on our catch. It had probably been attracted by the noise we were making and the smell of the fish debris thrown overboard. There might be others too lurking around for a feed.

The Creole French word for shark, "Reken! Reken!" was the cry all around the boat. Suddenly, instead of thinking about the red snapper supper we were looking forward to, there was a surge of activity as the idea of shark's fin soup replaced it. The guy who had claimed to be a jumbo jet pilot reacted first, by immediately deploying a rod with a mackerel as bait. As soon as it hit the water the bait was taken by the shark. This was exciting. The battle to bring the shark alongside the boat lasted some thirty minutes, until the shark had begun to get tired and less agitated. It was about six feet long, with deep, staring, hypnotic eyes glaring at us in the boat.

The idea was for the gillie to catch the leader line first, then tie a rope around its tail and drag the shark backwards with the boat. The effect of this is to reverse the water flow through the shark's gills and drown it. The shark, though, had other ideas, and with a last violent swirl of its head it broke the line and escaped. Gone were all the thoughts of shark steaks and shark's fin soup.

There was nothing left now to do but finish cleaning up the boat and make our way home, to Mahe and the mainland. However, while our gillie began washing down the now very treacherously wet deck and throwing fish waste overboard, wearing just flip flops, leaning over the boats edge to fill his bucket of water he slipped - and over the side he went. We had an emergency this time, and the cry came "Man overboard!" from everyone. The skipper, perched on his controls, knew what was going on. He immediately spun the boat round to return and collect our man overboard, but what followed once we had rescued him amazed us, bearing in mind what had just happened.

Our gillie, still in the shark-infested water, calmly removed his wrist watch, put it between his teeth above the waterline, and then started swimming for his lost hat, which by now was drifting away from the boat. Having retrieved it in a very matter of fact way, he swam to the boat, calmness personified, and clambered on board. Only then did he show what a frightening experience it had been for us all, and the swearing which followed would have made a pirate blush. He was a lucky man that day.

It was a day of vivid events to be remembered over the years and mulled over as we did frequently when Pierre, Andy and I found ourselves together over a glass of wine or two. It was a boatload of very tired but very satisfied fishermen who returned to the marina, where we had a reception on the quay from loads of relatives and friends anticipating a share of the day's catch. What a fantastic day it had been!

However, for Pierre, Andy and me, the edge was taken off that day by seeing a large fleet of Chinese and Japanese trawlers berthed with their miles and miles of netting. I found their fishing methods reprehensible as they were just plundering the ocean and severely depleting the stock of tuna and other species for their home market.

The Seychelles government has introduced a marine reservation nature reserve, with severe restrictions on coral diving and indiscriminate fishing. I just wish that it could stop, or at the very least curtail this large-scale fishing by foreign countries, from which the local population derives no benefit. The cavalier attitude to fishing by Japanese trawlers is fishing the ocean around the Seychelles to death. It is not too late to stop this madness.

For over two centuries, the islands have remained a melting pot of different races, traditions and religions from the four corners of the earth. In the evolution of its society, Seychelles has remained faithful to its multi-ethnic roots. Nearly every nation on earth has been represented in and influenced this melting pot of cultures, each one contributing their part to the people of the Seychelles Islands. This grand diversity of cultural influences and ethnic diversity has greatly inspired the level of racial harmony which remains the mainstay of today's vibrant yet tranquil nation for which this harmony is a way of life.

A helping hand
for my homeland

Today, I live in Hereford with my wife Barbara. About five years ago, I became involved with a local charity, known as the Hereford/Muheza Link Society, and I am a committee member. Ever since, every year I make a trip out to this local hospital in Tanzania, which I wholeheartedly support.

The charity was formed over twenty- five years ago, when three hospital-based consultants, working at the hospital in Hereford, created personal links with a Tanzanian hospital in Muheza, a busy little town about 20km inland from the coastal town of Tanga right in the north-eastern tip of Tanzania at the foothills of the Usambara Mountains. The creation of the charity formally recognised the developments of these primarily medical links.

The importance of this hospital is that it is at a major road junction around which the town of Muheza has grown, some six hours' travel by bus from the city of Dar es Salaam.

The actual hospital was known as Teule Hospital, but it has recently been renamed St Augustine Hospital by the new Bishop

Maimbo Mndolwa of Tanga. It is run by the Anglican church and relies heavily on charitable funding to continue its work.

Living in an area roughly one hundred by fifty kilometres, 280,000 people look to this hospital to provide them with primary health care. It is also a referral centre for 46 outlying village dispensaries and five health centres, with altogether over 200 beds. Two thirds of its population are Muslims and the government of Tanzania is Muslim-led.

The hospital itself typifies many rural African hospitals. There are two paediatric wards, two female and two male wards, one labour ward, a theatre, an X-ray department, a pharmacy and a laboratory. There are deficiencies in the provision of medical care, not only because of shortages of trained medical staff but also in support services necessary to help them to be effective. It is a familiar story across the region,

Common procedures include hernia repairs, caesarean sections, haemorrhoids and other bowel procedures. Orthopaedic procedures are common, due to the high road traffic accident rate. Travelling on public buses can be very dangerous in these parts. Most interesting is a weekly vesico-vaginal fistula operating list. These fistulas result from prolonged and obstructed labour, which can result in a hole between the vagina and bladder, meaning that women may continually leak small amounts of urine from the vagina.

The operation to repair these fistulas is not complicated, but it has infinite benefits to both women and the economy as these previously 'outcast' women are now able to rejoin society.

A key way in which the charity helps St Augustine hospital is in shipping containers to Muheza once or twice a year, with equipment and other medical items which are no longer usable in a modern NHS hospital but come in very handy in Muheza, considering their lack of funding and resources.

Filling either a twenty or forty-foot container could be wheelchairs, crutches, dressings, beds, trolleys, sutures and other sundries necessary to keep the hospital running as well as improving comforts and patients' lifestyles. Funding the container is very expensive for a charity that depends entirely on voluntary donations and subscriptions from its members. We depend on the generosity and kindness of the people in and around Herefordshire. Long may it continue.

The link encourages hospital staff exchanges. It invites four people, already working in various specialities in the hospital, to Hereford for a four week period working and observing in various departments. To qualify to make the journey here, they must also pass an interview in Muheza, speaking only in English for a five-minute period. I have invigilated at this interview, and it can prove very interesting to hear their goals and reasons for wanting to come to Hereford. This can be very difficult for many as Kiswahili is their first language, although English is widely spoken at the hospital.

Staff from Hereford hospital and surrounding areas are also encouraged to go for a sabbatical, but are self-funded. This provides staff with vital personal experience and training in the particular problems of providing medical care in a third-world hospital in rural Tanzania.

We could not run this very worthwhile scheme if we could not provide our African visitors with the air fares, their accommodation while in the UK and subsistence allowances. This all comes out of the charity's funds. The idea is that they return and teach their colleagues with what they have learnt over here.

It is like winning the lottery for many of them. Many go back with suitcases packed with clothing and other goodies. However, basic nurse pay is only around the equivalent of £300 per month. Consequently when visas are applied for the visitors to come to Hereford, the powers to be turn down 50% of all applicants, on the grounds of insufficient funds in their accounts. The authorities fear that they may just abscond and remain in the UK after their tour of duty. It is a problem which needs addressing, as each time a visa is applied for and turned down it costs our charity in the region of £80 or more, plus expenses. I wish I could find a way round this problem.

Unmentioned so far is the nurse's training school at St Augustine Hospital, with around 200 students, which the charity supports by assisting with tutors' and medical officers' training. This school has been renamed St Augustine's Institute of Health Science by the new bishop and accordingly, they have a vision of becoming a university sometime in the future. Now that's what I call a visionary outlook.

I usually time my annual visit to the arrival of a container, which we previously packed in Hereford. They can take anything up to five months to arrive from the UK, hopefully around January, the hottest time of the year, as this is also the mango and pineapple season. I wouldn't miss it for the world. While I'm there I base myself in the operating theatres, teaching, mentoring and supporting the theatre staff. As a committee member I also troubleshoot problems in other areas of the hospital. I feel highly motivated in helping the hospital, as I feel this is the way I can best help the country I grew up in. Being able to speak the local language, Kiswahili, allows me to talk easily with all the staff, so I hear and discuss more of their problems and requests, as well as complaints. The staff there relate to me as a medical person who shares their language.

Over the time I have spent in Muheza, I feel that my relationships with the staff have matured into trust. This has allowed me to appreciate social issues as well as medical ones that I can sometimes do something to overcome.

When off duty, the members of the staff of the nursing school organise and take part in team games. This is fun when kicking a ball about on the practice field, but when they were representing the hospital against local teams in football or netball, their style was cramped because they had no team outfits in which to play. This was solved initially by good friends of mine Peter and Kay in Hereford, who funded the purchase of a set for the footballers, which was shared by the girls' netball team. Two for the price of one. My luggage allowance and bulging suitcase, was overlooked by a kind airline check in girl at the airport.

It was extremely rewarding and motivating to see the lads, some may I add physically and athletically built, squeezing into the shirts, in Barcelona colours, for their first match in proper kits. They invited me to their first away match, which they duly won. Pictures of that event adorn the nursing school walls.

Their victory must have been inspired by wearing proper football strip for the first time. I now hear the kit has passed its usefulness and the team need replacements.

My last report will gladly say that the Fownhope Football Club, a village just on the outskirts of Hereford, under the presidency of kind-hearted men by the name of Dennis Beavan and chairman Roy Ovel, has donated enough strips and kit to support up to four complete teams, including shirts for the girls' netball teams, so they do not have to share the kit any more. This went to Tanzania on the June 2013 container and has since arrived safely at the school of nursing. My prayers have been answered. I can't wait to see the green colours of Fownhope Football Club on African backs when I visit them next. It shows that there are still very generous and willing people in our community, willing to help good causes.

The hospital, I feel, has many issues and problems in terms of electricity, water, funding and hospital management. Every day a power cut occurs, which could last two to three hours, sometimes more, thus curtailing operating sessions.

To illustrate how problems interlink consider the following situations.

The water source is a borehole down a steep ravine behind the hospital, some 500 metres or so. A Hereford member of the Link is a plumber who, at his own expense and time, like other members travelling there, has tried to extend the water supply to several areas and wards of the hospital. This was successfully accomplished, much to his credit, but subsequently, circumstances have had a habit of thwarting the effectiveness of his work.

Another attempt to provide a proper installation to provide the hospital with water was funded by the Rotary Club in Hereford a few years ago. The pumping system has not performed as anticipated for unknown reasons, not helped by inadequate understanding or maintenance of the system. The lack of powerful pumps to provide the hospital, which is on a steep embankment, plus the fact that burst pipes occur along the cultivated route, does not help. This superficially-laid pipe passes through a plot of land which is dug by pickaxes and shovels by the locals growing their crops. It is not laid deep enough to prevent accidents such as burst pipes. I know this for a fact, as my storekeeper friend and I have walked the distance, in the heat of the day, in my determination to grasp and understand the problem.

Large areas of lush growth along the submerged pipes confirm the leakage of water. The hospital has recently installed large water tanks at the end of each ward building in an attempt to capture and store rainwater from the roofs during the rainy season.

Each area of the hospital has an industrial generator to provide energy when electricity fails. They do not have the necessary funds to buy fuel to operate these generators. It is an ever-recurring problem and source of complaint, and sometimes excuses, as to why things don't work.

The local electrical and mechanical engineer on site is not properly trained to sort out the problem, although he has visited Hereford three times over the years to gain experience.

No electricity or water means no operating or, at the very least, curtailed schedules. This in return affects the income generated, as they charge for all operations, treatments and drugs issued. This then affects funds. The complaint is always that no money is available for repairs. It is a vicious circle that has to be broken to be improved.

Operating instruments and sundries certainly need updating and are scarce. The hospital staff do their best to make a success of the hospital, but are too frightened to speak out and complain about issues that are present. Weak local hospital management does not help.

Newborn babies are wrapped up in very distinctive and colourful local materials known as "kangas". This cloth is worn by all women in Tanzania, and is their national dress. There are no identifying bracelets used, as we do in our NHS maternity units, to identify name and date of birth. However each mother can identify their newborn babies by their own distinctive colour kangas. On laundry days the grass areas outside the labour wards are awash with bright colours from the day's washing.

There is a European-style bungalow within the hospital grounds, built by a kind retired doctor living in Herefordshire, to accommodate European visitors to the hospital, which fills up very quickly, so it is not often available to stay. There is also a very small basic four-roomed hostel within the hospital grounds for overseas medical students to live in while attending their secondments and further training at the hospital. This is a major income generator for our Link, as they are billed for their duration and training. This very welcome extra money is used to provide help in the hospital education funds.

Hospital students from all over the world, as far as Australia, New Zealand and the USA, including the UK attend for a six weeks period. Placement are highly sought for, and are based on a first come, first served basis for the 5-6 places available.

Lack of facilities in terms of electricity, running water and maintenance make it just bearable to live in. To save water a basic rule is applied – 'If it's yellow, let it mellow, if it's brown, flush it down'.

Working at St Augustine Hospital certainly holds challenges. However, it is an exciting and rewarding area of Tanzania to visit.

Tanga city is today the fourth largest city in Tanzania with the second largest port, and is considered to be the best planned in the country. It has a wealth of architectural history, with historic buildings of style and design from the period of Germanic rule. The style of the buildings now to be seen in Tanga harks back to the time when Tanzania was a German colony a century ago, which strongly influenced their architecture. It is beautiful beyond imagination and really worth visiting. However, their cultural significance has only recently begun to be recognised by the local government agencies, which, primarily for economic reasons, have allowed many of the buildings to deteriorate to their present state. Fortunately the example of Zanzibar, which has encouraged tourism to very good effect, has shown the need to preserve local heritage. There are many places of interest to visit, natural heritage, historical sites, cultural activities and the welcoming ambience of the people makes it worth visiting and staying.

The Department of Antiquities in Tanga has been urged by the locals to protect the many old buildings and other historical sites in the region, for them to be good tourist attractions. A wide range of tourism exists, from the scenic Usambara mountain range, lush tropical forest of Armani nature reserve, natural attractions and marvellous beaches, to enchanting culture and history. This department has already taken steps to preserve Tongoni, an ancient village, and the famous Amboni Caves, both just outside Tanga. Other historical sites where there are mosques and houses built by Shiraz merchants during the 4th and 5th centuries are also receiving attention. Tanga, in its earlier days, became the largest producer and exporter of sisal in the world.

When I visit Tanzania I live in Tanga, some 23 kilometres away from the hospital in the Lutheran Mission Station, which provides clean, safe and cheap accommodation in an area known as Razkazoni.

I stay and pay my own way and accommodation in Tanga because the options in Muheza are unsuitable. I commute on a daily basis, using the local small minibuses called "Dhalla Dhalla."

Sharing a twenty-seated bus, with bald tyres, reckless drivers, some chickens, bags of mangoes, mattresses, bananas, water buckets and fifty other locals crammed in the back is fascinating. I never get tired of the journey.

One of the pleasures of staying in Tanga for a month is that there is time to find interesting places to eat local good meals at local prices. One of my favourite and, as it happens most quirky, restaurants is on the high ground overlooking the harbour of Tanga. It is in the town centre and is run and owned by a pleasant Indian couple and their son. The main kitchen was once a container in a car park at the back of the restaurant building. It had windows cut out as serving hatches. For a long time, for obvious reasons, it was known as the "container restaurant", but times have changed and the new kitchen is now part of the restaurant building. Now known as the "Sea View Restaurant", it offers some of the best food in the area, particularly their lovely fresh-caught king prawn curries. People from miles around come to this restaurant to enjoy their other specialities on the menu.

Whenever I visit Tanzania now, I like to rest for a few days after the long flight to wander around Dar es Salaam and renew my long-standing acquaintance with friends I have made, and the city sights which bring back many memories of days in our youth. To stay in, I have found an excellent Italian-run Non-Governmental Organisation hostel called Cefa House in the Mikocheni 'B' area of Dar. It is cheap, clean, safe and offers value for money. Part of their income is used to support good causes and several charities in Tanzania. It has fourteen en suite rooms with dining facilities.

I find this place matches my aspirations and feelings about charity and the proper use of resources to benefit those in the world who really need them. The work at the hospital I find very frustrating, with two steps forward and one back, but very rewarding nevertheless. I see my birthplace and heritage deteriorating because of neglect and corruption in all walks of life. Whenever I travel through the Tanzanian countryside, wherever there were animals and wildlife, I do not see them now. Where are they? Ironically I see more wildlife, like deer, foxes and pheasants while travelling around the UK. I haven't seen a wild boar yet, but I live in hope.

Africa needs help, from technology, to feed itself without destroying itself in the process, but its image in the world of corruption is holding it to ransom. I see all the personal motivations at work in the Tanzanian society I inhabit. At least I have the consolation that I know there are solutions to all its problems, but none of them can be resolved without persistence, and my efforts are, in a very small way, somewhere turning a mere existence into a life.

A century ago, Tanzania was a German colony, and in an earlier chapter, we noted that it became a British colony in 1916. However, I did not mention what happened in 1914 when a British force tried and failed to take over the German colony. This chapter remedies this omission.

By and large, to the British people, WW1 was mainly fought in Europe, with episodes in Turkey and the Middle East. To Tanzanians, it might be said their clearest recollection of the war was a battle that was directed at capturing the seaport of Tanga so as to take over German East Africa.

This became known as the Battle of the Bees, for these insects played a part in helping to defeat a British Indian Expeditionary Force under Major General A. E. Aitkin. This saw the British defeated by a significantly smaller but better trained force of Germans, local Askari soldiers and colonial volunteers.

The British resolve to capture German East Africa was to be implemented with an amphibious attack on Tanga. However, it turned into a debacle.

On 2 November 1914, almost three months after its creation and planning, the British ship HMS *Fox*, as part of a British task force, arrived off Tanga. The inner harbour was relatively shallow and protected by the Tanga Peninsula and Toten Island. Tanga, at that time, consisted of about 900 houses, with larger well-built stone houses along the waterfront. Behind them the town was divided by the Usambara Railway into the native quarter and the European settlement.

Dense vegetation surrounded the town. Tanga was about ten meters above sea level and its port had a rudimentary jetty without any loading cranes. The inner harbour was too shallow for large ships to dock at the jetty, so the ships had to be unloaded by lighters in the harbour.

East of the town, towards the Tanga Peninsula, there was a relatively flat coastal plain covered with thick, dense vegetation which changed in character south of the Askari road to cultivated rubber trees - and apiaries buzzing with African bees.

Tanga Peninsula ends in cliffs rising twenty to thirty meters above small, muddy, beaches along the Indian Ocean. The beaches on the eastern edge of the peninsula were sandwiched between the cliffs and partially-submerged mangrove swamps.

As the sixteen ships of the task force anchored off Tanga, the cruiser HMS *Fox* began moving into the harbour. The *Fox* was unable to reach the inner harbour until 0700, as fear of mines and German removal of all the navigation aids slowed the ship. The ship's captain, commander F. W. Caulfield, went ashore, giving Tanga one hour to surrender and take down the imperial flag. Before departing, he demanded to know if the harbour had been mined. It was not, but he was assured it was.

This gave time for the relatively few soldiers of the Schutz Truppe and the citizens of Tanga to prepare for an attack. The German commander, Lt. Col. Paul Emil Lettow-Vorbeck rushed to Tanga from Moshi, by rail, a distance of around 360 kilometres. He took charge of the operation, with initially only a single company of Askaris, with further troops eventually brought in by rail from Moshi, numbering about a thousand, in six companies. However, before that, the British Commander, Lt Gen Aitken, began the unopposed landing of the British force and supplies in the harbour.

Many of the British-led troops were Indian peasant conscripts, pulled from their homes, given rudimentary training, and embarked on troopships. Aitken had great faith in them. However, these were not the justly-famous Gurkhas and Sikh warriors who were trained to the standards of the Old Contemptibles. For the past three weeks they had been crammed in the holds of the ships, inactive and seasick. They were not at their fighting best.

Fierce fighting broke out, initially in jungle skirmishes, and after bitter street fighting by the harbour contingent force of the Gurkhas of the Kashmiri Rifles and the 2nd Royal North Lancashire Regiment, they made good progress, entered the town and ran up the Union Jack. Less well trained, and equipped, battalions of the Imperial Service Brigade scattered and ran away from the battle.

Then, as the 98th Infantry attempted to advance, it was attacked by swarms of angry African bees. The African honey bee responds quickly to disturbances by people or animals, sometimes in excess of 50 feet from the nest. They can even sense vibrations from power equipment a hundred feet from the nest. African honey bees can chase a disturbance up to a mile or more. Their defensive behaviour is an evolutionary response to their many biological competitors, including honey badgers, bee eaters and even humans, in their native range.

Within moments of the bees' attack, the 98th Infantry was

scattered in every direction along the plateau overlooking the harbour front and was broken up. The bees attacked the Germans as well, hence the battle's nickname.

British propaganda transformed the bee interlude into a fiendish German plot, conjuring up hidden trip wires along the plateau of Tanga to agitate the hives situated all along the harbourside.

The German reinforcements arrived by rail and Lettow-Vorbeck ordered his troops to envelope the British flank and rear by launching bayonet attacks, along the entire front to bugle cries and piercing tribal war chants. A furious and frustrated General Aitken ordered a general withdrawal back to the ships.

The German Captain, Baumstark, explained the situation to Von Lettow-Vorbeck, but could neither confirm nor deny if the British had occupied Tanga after the withdrawal. Von Lettow-Vorbeck immediately conducted a personal reconnaissance of Tanga on a bicycle. He discovered that Tanga was unoccupied.

This shows the strategic difference between the two men, Paul Emil von Lettow Vorbeck for Germany, and Arthur Edward Aitken for Britain. One of these preparations was not reconnaissance; Aitken failed to order any reconnaissance towards Tanga. Lack of planning and preparation make for piss-poor performance, as in this case.

The only thing left to do after this ignominious withdrawal, during which all the British supplies landed were left behind, was to take care of the wounded. The two Generals met and arrangements were decided over a bottle of brandy, and a number of casualties were transferred from the local hospital to the ships, where they could be better cared for. They both compared battle notes and strategies after the British had raised their white flag.

But the Germans did get to keep more than just their sea port. Because the British had surrendered, they were required to leave their supplies on the battlefield, so the British left behind nearly all their equipment, giving the Germans 600,000 rounds of ammunition, plus machine guns and rifles.

With this done, Force 'B', led by HMS *Fox*, slinked away from Tanga and steamed back to Mombasa. The operation was an utter disaster for the British, who suffered 817 casualties out of a force of 8,000. German casualties amounted to only 16 Europeans and 48 Askaris out of a force of approximately 1,000. The casualty toll, perhaps, gives a better impression of the disaster that befell this ill-planned and even worse realisation of this colonial expedition.

The outcome for the two generals involved was only too predictable. For Aitken it signalled the end of his career. His failure earned him a reduction in rank to colonel, retirement and being placed on half-pay for the remainder of the war. Von Lettow-Vorbeck and his Schutztruppe fared better.

Although the concept of joint operations was in its infancy, Aitken could also have made much better use of the fire support available from HMS Fox in the execution of his assault. As it was, Caufield, the captain of HMS *Fox*, appeared ambivalent about the notion of doing anything more than sweeping the harbour of suspected mines.

Finally, Aitken's arrogance, especially the capabilities of his own Indian troops versus those of the German Askaris, was another contributing factor to the defeat. In short, Aitken's flawed leadership and poor generalship were what ultimately led to the debacle at Tanga.

Lettow-Vorbeck was able to rearm three Askari companies with modern rifles, and remained undefeated. General Lettow Vorbeck's reputation, already in the ascendant, continued to grow. His war record was indeed remarkable, as he never lost a battle and remained undefeated by the time he eventually "surrendered" to the British on 25th November 1918, having belatedly heard of the Armistice from a captured British prisoner. He returned to Germany a national hero.

Estimated British killed were two thousand men. The large island off the harbour, known today as Toten or dead men's island, remains a war grave, and is not visited by tourist.

The magnificent but now run-down hospital built over one hundred years ago by the Germans still stands in the grounds of the only local hospital site, Bombo in Tanga. The town of Tanga remains greatly influenced by the German East African rule today.

At the scene of this early colonial battle for the town of Tanga a memorial clock tower was later built to commemorate those who had died and are buried close by. Today, it is overrun and the tower dilapidated, with the clock face gone. It should be restored as a dedication to the British and Indian troops who, once again, fought for our cause in East Africa.

Farewell to a beloved brother

For the last few years of my brother Pierre's life, he and his wife Nina lived in Lagos, Portugal, where Nina still remains. Pierre was enjoying his boating and fishing and we kept in touch, with the occasional visit. We enjoyed each other's company immensely, eating and drinking late into the night. He and Nina had renovated an old town house within the ancient walls of the town. He was extremely proud to show off this outstanding project, and would tell you in every detail all the aspects of it.

Pierre had acquired an ex-US navy fast rescue boat and named her *Ninadee*. He was very proud of his boat and the speed she achieved around Lagos waters, and tells of stories of rescuing other sailors and boat men, in trouble along the Lagos shores. He enjoyed fishing trips with friends.

Two years ago we met up at the biannual OTT Reunited held in Coventry. This is a well-run and meaningful organisation run by and for retired ex-servicemen and women who served in the Royal Army Medical Corp as operating theatre technicians now also known informally as "the diminishing Band of Brothers". We meet old buddies and friends with whom we had served with or heard of in our military careers and provide help to charities as well as members if and when required. Here we have good food, wine and conversation and try to remember old colleagues who have passed on. Pierre was of course the centre of attraction and rightful admiration by all his comrades.

This was one of the last places I saw Pierre. His health, although he was only 67 years of age, was beginning to deteriorate. He was suffering from diabetes, and had had to have his big toe amputated. He made very good progress and recovered very well from this. Unfortunately his heart and coronary arteries were troubling him and he did have heart attacks, which he recovered from after being treated by the doctors in Portugal.

He was evacuated, by the air ambulance, to Lisbon from his home, for emergency assessment and treatment during one of his bad heart attack. He underwent a triple heart bypass operation by the cardiologist at Lisbon and was recovering well.

He was discharged home with great relief some few weeks later and appeared to be making very good progress. Whenever I rang and spoke to him he always said, "Yes, doing OK and recovering Bruv, onwards and upwards." His mood was buoyant.

Then, out of the blue in the early hours of one morning, we received the news from a distraught Nina to say that Pierre passed away in her arms. It was the 6th October 2012. I was shocked and devastated.

Only a few days earlier we had heard of his good progress, so this shocking turn of events was very hard to believe and accept. I can't get over it and I don't think I ever will. I have lost a beloved brother, and I still cannot take it all in. My greatest sympathy and condolences go out to Nina and their daughters Juliette, Ginette, Nicola and Alison, and all their grandchildren. God bless you all.

Pierre's funeral was held at the beautiful Catholic church at Praia la Ruiz, a seaside town on the outskirts of Lagos, in Portugal. Pierre's coffin was draped with the Royal Army Medical Corps flag with its distinctive band of cherry red, royal blue and old gold colours of our Corps. A true military hero and a champion man in all ways.

The organist was none other than his old mate and band member of "The Rough Diamond" of Hong Kong and Berlin fame and a close family friend ex OTT, Tony Sisley.

This is what Tony Sisley had to say about his friend Pierre:

I first met Pierre in the spring of 1971 when I was posted to the British Military Hospital in Hong Kong. I had heard of a BMH Hong Kong band called the Rough Diamonds in which Pierre played the guitar and sang, but I wasn't aware that I had been volunteered in advance to join them on my arrival in the so-called Pearl of the Orient.

But orders are orders, and Adrian "Black Mac" MacDonald, also an operating theatre technician, together with Big John Mills, both of Rough Diamonds, came up to the bar at the military hospital on the evening of my arrival to make the necessary arrangements for me to join them.

Little did they know that their newest recruit was nowhere near the bar (well, of course!) as he was starting to explore the delights of his new posting and getting up to as much mischief as possible, sadly without much success!

However, all was finalised the following evening and yours truly met Pierre for the first time, playing the keyboards with Rough Diamonds that very weekend, in fact before even starting work in the operating theatres.

Such were the priorities of the time.

When Pierre and his family left Hong Kong, Rough Diamonds continued successfully but it really wasn't the same without him.

I was posted from Hong Kong to the British military hospital in Berlin and you can imagine my delight on hearing one day that in a few weeks' time a certain Peter Herlick Rene Naya was being posted in. Needless to say theatre duties assumed a secondary role as Pierre and I reformed Rough Diamonds.

In addition to the unforgettable memory of having worked with Pierre both in the operating theatres and playing in Rough Diamonds, I shall never forget the warm welcome extended to me in both Hong Kong and Berlin from the whole family when I was able to visit them.

I was usually greeted at the door by a vocal quartet of little girls addressing me formally Rat Bag!

This warm welcome, without exception, always included being fed and watered.

Having flown in to Lagos, Portugal, on the eve of Pierre's funeral and nearing the hotel close to ten in the night, in the shuttle bus I received a call from Juliette, his eldest daughter, saying that it wouldn't be a good idea to come to the house that evening as, understandably, Nina was extremely tired.

Someone, however would come to the hotel shortly after my arrival to collect from me the RAMC corps flag, as this had to be delivered to the funeral directors early the following morning. It then occurred to me that this would be the first time in history to visit the Nayas territory without being offered food and drink.

Juliette, her husband Raf, and Nicola arrived at the hotel and, needless to say, we had a couple of jars and a good chat, during which I noticed that Raf had brought a carrier bag which he handed to me. Surprise, surprise this contained a goodly portion of Nina's curry of the day, plus fork, bottle of beer and bottle opener.

This proved that the Naya welcoming hospitality tradition was not broken.

I shall never forget Pierre, Nina and the girls, and will never be able to dismiss from my mind that on that evening, with so much to occupy her mind, Nina somehow managed to think of an ageing hungry traveller in need of a quality repast.

Well, Pierre, I can't imagine the good Lord allowing you to rest in too much peace, as he'll surely be putting you to work in the celestial music department.

Whether or not an electric guitar, amplifier and microphone can be plugged in up there is also uncertain (it could be a current problem- sorry!) so be prepared to start learning the harp.

God bless you and keep you, dear friend."

I must thank Tony for this, which brings tears of memories to my eyes. I wish he was still here with us all.

Another was from John Mills, ex-rhythm guitarist of the Rough Diamonds in Hong Kong and now living in Australia. He very recently sent me a message, when I was undertaking this venture of writing this book. This is what he said:

It was a complete shock to learn of Pierre's passing. Of all the band members he was the most domesticated, and apart from our drummer Neil Hardcastle he was the baby. It would look good in your book for me to reveal salacious details of his exploits, but unfortunately he was not that type. Even his jokes were toned down to a gentleman level, giggling at the most innocent double entendre and becoming quite embarrassed by the possible meaning.

After completing a gig he would head off home without detouring to some of Mac's and my more questionable haunts, preferring instead to head off home to his beloved wife and 'gals'. He never deviated from this in all the time I knew him. The only time I remember him getting excited was when we were booked to appear on TV. Yes, your brother was a TV star! He even polished up his white Burns guitar to look like Hank Marvin. I trust that the family will treasure this much-loved instrument. When I get home today I will endeavour to find and scan for you the newspaper report of our moment of TV glory. I am going to the Seychelles in September and will be thinking of my friend Pierre and will end with one of Pierre's goodbyes 'God Bless'".

Well John did find some classic band photos and memorabilia for me, and I thank him sincerely for that.

Joe D'Silva, who now lives in Canada, says:

"Thank you so much for your touching story and sad news about your brother Pierre, a classmate of mine all those years ago in Dar es Salaam. In Dar we were really good friends, especially during the school holidays. After school we used to go raiding for mangoes and guavas. Mostly it was just joking and fooling around, and boy was he ever the very best at relating funny stories to us boys. Our house used to be a meeting place for all us kids, as we had three guitarists, Pierre, my brother Olly and Patrick Gobbin. We used to have a ball after our football games. One afternoon during our Christmas break the six of us chums went looking for ripe mangoes. Behind the Palm Beach Hotel, not far from our house in the Upanga area of Dar, there was a tree full of delicious large mangoes. So your brother Pierre, Norman Fernandes and I climbed up this very large tree and shook the branches and a whole lot of mangoes fell to the ground, where the other three were picking up the ripe ones and leaving the raw ones behind. Suddenly out of nowhere the African man who was the sentry of the property came to catch us all in action. The others ran away and we were asked to climb down from the tree and collect all the raw mangoes. There must have been at least about 100 mangoes. He wanted us to pay twenty shillings for them or we had to eat them all and not go until we had done so. Do you know how dreadful it is to eat even 10 raw mangoes? So there we were eating the raw mangoes by force, one by one for a good hour. Meantime, a distant friend passing by managed to convince the sentry to let us go by giving him 5 shillings which he had in his pocket. That was the last time we ever climbed mango trees.

Pierre, your brother, surely proved to be a heroic soldier and medic, and we kind of feel certain pride of having been one of his young buddies. Ever so sorry for your loss."

It was fitting that a letter of condolence was read out in church from none other than Simon Weston OBE, the Falklands War veteran, who Pierre did meet on various documentary programmes. It brought tears to every eye present.

It was remarkable how a very bright, intense, orange beam of light shone just on his coffin in church during the sad ceremony through a small window in the church. In a way I like to think that Pierre was there with us. This light brought us all great comfort.

I only wish he was here with me as I try to write this, and just hope I have done him some justice. If I have missed anything out, I am sorry bruv.

I have just returned from one of my charity trips to Dar es Salaam. While there I was constantly reminded of the places we frequented some fifty years earlier. At certain times I was in tears. The trip gave me great inspirations for this book in memory of Pierre, a loved brother I had lost. Pierre was with me all the way. He would have had so much more to give.

One of the highlights was to have a holy mass and light a few candles at St Joseph's Cathedral, where we were baptised and attended holy mass as Catholics growing up in that wonderful city with heaps of memories. I know Pierre was with me, because as I lit the candles in his memory, not only did the church bells ring, not having been heard for almost 50 years, but that same bright beam of intense light shone again through the church's windows over the candles. I am sure he has got a rock band going in the skies up above.

I recently attended our OTT Reunion gathering and was approached by many people, especially ex-colleagues of Pierre, offering their condolences. He had made many good friends during his life in the army and in retirement. Pierre was revered and loved by all in the Medical Corps and remembered for his achieving one of the highest award for bravery, the Military Medal.

One particular early colleague of Pierre, all those many years ago, while he was undergoing his OTT training in Colchester military hospital, was Ted Richards. He was the Warrant Officer way back in the mid-sixties era who trained and mentored Pierre during his training period there. He was extremely sad to hear of his passing, but also very proud to have known and trained Pierre. He was immensely proud also that he had gained the Military Medal in the Falklands War. This very same chap totally diversified after leaving the forces to make Colchester his home town and opened a delicatessen shop in Crouch Street and learnt to speak Mandarin.

It was the very same shop that mother used to frequent, at times taking me with her to do her spice shopping.

Ted had a thriving business and made a success of it. It was a pleasure speaking to him and listening to his fondness and pride for Pierre. That's what mates are all about.

I miss my brother and for sure we will meet again sometime. I have had to endure many moments of anguish and emotion in writing this book and telling the whole world about our story, and in particular, that of Pierre. It has not been easy. However I was determined to tell his story in this fashion, and just hope I have done him proud. There were many times when I thought that Pierre was with me all along the way looking after, and guiding me.

We can shed tears that he has gone

or we can smile because he has lived.

We can close our eyes and pray he'll come back

or we can open our eyes and see all he has left.

Our hearts can be empty because we can't see him

Or we can be full of the love that we shared.

We can turn our backs on tomorrow and live yesterday

Or we can be happy for tomorrow because of yesterday.

We can remember him only that he has gone

Or we can cherish his memory and let it live on.

We can cry and close our minds, be empty and
turn our backs

Or we do what he would want, smile, open our eyes,
love and go on.

THE END

ND - #0439 - 270225 - C28 - 229/152/24 - PB - 9781861512413 - Matt Lamination